EXPLORING THE THA
Wallingford, C
and the Upper Thames

EXPLORING
THE THAMES VALLEY
Wallingford, Oxford
and the Upper Thames

Tom Lawrence

With Historical Notes

COUNTRYSIDE BOOKS
NEWBURY, BERKSHIRE

Based upon the author's
Thames Valley volume
in the 'Walks for Motorists' series
originally published by Frederick Warne Ltd.

This book published 1990
© Tom Lawrence 1990

COUNTRYSIDE BOOKS
3 Catherine Road
Newbury, Berkshire

ISBN 185306 103 4

Cover photograph of The Thames at Hampton Court
taken by David Sharp

Produced through MRM Associates Ltd., Reading
Typeset by Acorn Bookwork, Salisbury
Printed in England by J. W. Arrowsmith Ltd., Bristol

Contents

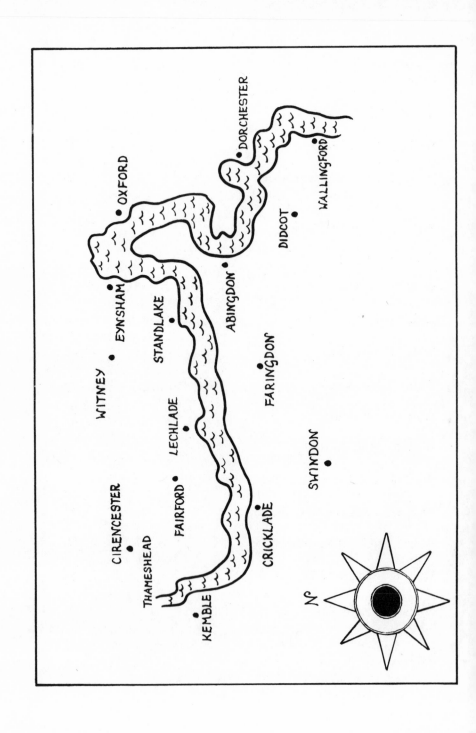

Introduction

All the walks in this book, and its companion volume, have been planned to include a section of the Thames towpath, or riverside path, in an upstream direction. Each walk is complete in itself and they need not be undertaken in any particular order. Yet the basic idea of the two books is that if you walk all 30 routes in sequence you will gain a sense of exploring the whole of the river from Kingston, on the outskirts of London, to Thames Head, its source in a Gloucestershire meadow.

The first volume brought us from Kingston to Goring. With this second volume we explore the river from South Stoke, a village not far from Goring, to the source. The scenery which unfolds before us as we travel with this book in hand is less dramatic than that which the first book revealed – there is nothing comparable with the hanging woods of Cliveden or the precipitous Goring Gap – yet is none the worse for that. We shall see Dorchester and Abingdon, pleasant towns both, and Oxford, and thereafter all is peace and tranquillity until Lechlade is reached, and again until we come to Cricklade. Indeed, between Godstow just north of Oxford, and Lechlade, no village, let alone a town, lies on the river's banks. A constant feature of almost every scene is the endless variety of trees, forming patterns against the sky and reflecting in the water to leave a lasting memory of beauty. Yet there is much more than the river itself to be enjoyed on every one of our walks as our circular routes take us along field-paths, through woods and over hills.

The course of the Thames has not always been the one we follow in these books. Once upon a time the river flowed into the Wash but when the glacial formations in the last Ice Age pushed it south it steadily bored a way through the chalk of the Chilterns and carved the Goring Gap. Earlier still, when the North Sea was land, the Thames was but a tributary of the Rhine.

We walk with history, too, there being, especially, reminders of the tragic Civil War in the ancient bridges which were fiercely fought over, the church in which Cromwell stabled his horses during the siege of Royalist Wallingford and the bridge from which he watched the cruel beheading of the entire garrison when its castle eventually surrendered. We pass the spot where Matilda, daughter of Henry I and rightful Queen of England, fled across the frozen Thames. And we see the ruins of the nunnery where the good sisters cherished the 'Fair Rosamund', mistress of Henry II, later murdered ('tis said) by the queen.

Because of its unspoilt, typically English (although in no small measure, man-made) scenery the Thames has long been popular for pleasure tripping. The excursions to Oxford, run by an enterprising Abingdon trader in 1555 to witness the burning at the stake of Bishops Latimer and Ridley were by no means the first examples of pleasure boating on the river. Today, the constant movement of countless brightly painted pleasure craft adds colour to the enchantment of the scene.

Although the river has been navigated by barges since Saxon times, carrying goods between London and Oxford and beyond, its heyday as an artery of trade was, perhaps, in the Middle Ages. Craft were then hauled by gangs of labourers called halers while, over the long stretches that lacked a towpath, they were pushed along by the boatmen, wielding lengthy poles. With the coming of canals in the late 18th century the river became an important navigation within the inland waterway network. The Thames and Severn Canal joined it above Lechlade in 1789, the Oxford Canal linked it to the Midlands and the North a year later, and the Basingstoke Canal, which connected to the Thames through the river Wey at Weybridge, was opened in 1796. Navigational improvements were then urgently demanded, particularly the provision of pound locks to replace the old 'flash' locks – dangerous, wasteful of water and ever a source of acrimony between boatmen and millers – and a continuous towpath for the horses that were now beginning to be used for drawing the vessels.

A continuous towpath was more easily demanded than provided. Although Thames Commissioners were now in charge where administration had been almost non-existent before, formidable problems reared. The shallows, islands and muddy banks of a natural river, developments on the waterside and, not least, the intransigence of riparian landowners who refused to have a towpath on their land (or demanded exorbitant tolls if they did) all meant that a towpath had to be constructed sometimes on one bank and sometimes on the other. Numerous ferries, often with only a short distance between them, were therefore needed to take men and horses across, adding time and cost to every journey. Now that commercial traffic has died, the barges, horses and boatmen have all gone, and the ferries, too.

The locks remain, of course, and the cottages beside them. Whether modern or a century old these lock-keepers' residences are always pleasing in appearance while their gardens are invariably beautifully tended and a delight to the eye when we reach them.

The National Rivers Authority (Thames Region) is responsible for the management of water resources, pollution control, land drainage, flood defences, fish stocks, conservation and much else, including recreational uses. It welcomes considerate walkers to its towpaths, as it does anglers and birdwatchers, also. Not every length of towpath is a right of way but every length followed on our walks, if not a right of way, is a permissive way. Similarly, when we are walking inland from the river on our circular routes all our itineraries utilise public rights of way as designated on the Ordnance Survey maps with the exception of one or two paths which are permissive ways. Nevertheless, it must always be remembered that the waterside terrain and the farmland or woodland through which our paths pass are private property and should be treated with proper respect and consideration.

The numbers of the Ordnance Survey 1:50,000 sheet, or sheets, which cover the area are given in the 'How to Get There' section of each walk, together with the Grid Reference of the starting point. The sketch maps provided should be adequate but a full map undeniably adds interest to a walk and allows distant features to be identified.

Footwear is an important element in a walker's equipment. For most of our walks stout shoes should be adequate but boots (worn with two pairs of thick socks) are better and even wellies in wet seasons may not be out of place. Although mud is likely to be encountered on any walk anywhere, the Thames Valley seems to have more than its fair share.

Always interpret my directions with discretion, for paths may be diverted, hedges removed, gates fall down, signs may disappear and almost anything can be eroded by vandals. One of their favourite tricks, by the way, is to turn a signpost round to face the wrong way, if they can. That said, none of the rambles should present any real difficulties. The most vexing problem likely to be encountered is finding a path across a field has been ploughed up. Or, worse, that it has not only been ploughed up but crops are growing upon it. Don't worry. Although a farmer has a right to plough a path, except for one that follows the side of a field, generally he has an obligation to make good the surface of the path within two weeks of ploughing. Unhappily, many of them are contemptuous of this duty. If you come to a path that has been ploughed up and not reinstated you may tread it out. Similarly, if the path has been planted you may walk its line through the crop, but do it in single file. Usually, there is no difficulty in seeing where the line of a path runs; it is almost always straight towards the gate or stile to be seen on the opposite side of the field. Remember – if, for fear of following the line of a right of way through a field of waving corn you go round the edge of the field you are going where you have no right to go; are trespassing, in fact.

The timings quoted in the 'Distance' section of each walk represent **my** actual walking time. You may walk faster than I do, for I confess I am a fairly slow walker. You must allow more time if you intend to visit pubs and/or churches, to picnic or loiter at locks to watch the boats go through. Many of the churches you may wish to visit you will find locked, a sad reflection upon the times we live in. I have observed, too, that nowadays it is becoming increasingly rare to find a friendly note pinned up in the porch of a church saying where the key may be obtained. Yet enquiries will generally lead to the key's whereabouts.

A long-distance waterside route is at present being established all the way from the Thames Barrier at Greenwich to Thames Head, largely through the initiative of the Ramblers' Association. Under the auspices of the Countryside Commission the Thames Path will, it is expected, be officially opened around 1995.

If you feel ready to stride out on 175 miles of lineal walking, you will need a guide entitled *The Thames Walk*. It is written and illustrated by the man who, since the beginning, has been the chief driving force in this admirable enterprise, David Sharp. *The Thames Walk* (new edition 1990) is published by the Ramblers' Association, price £2.95.

The circular rambles in this book, together with those in its companion volume, will give you an enjoyable sense of exploring the Thames from Kingston to its source. Yet we do it only by taking short samples. Our walks, on which we follow selected lengths of Thames-side paths in an upstream direction take in some of the loveliest stretches of the riverside and its surrounding glorious countryside. I have had great pleasure in preparing these walks. I hope you will gain as much enjoyment from them as I have.

Tom Lawrence
May 1990

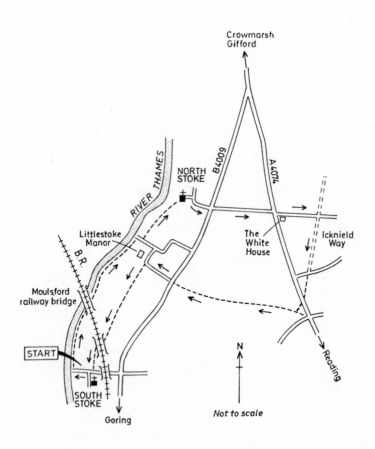

Crowmarsh
Gifford

RIVER THAMES

NORTH
STOKE

B4009

A4074

Littlestoke
Manor

The
White
House

Icknield
Way

B.R.

Moulsford
railway bridge

START

SOUTH
STOKE

Goring

Reading

N

Not to scale

South Stoke

Introduction: This is a walk on which we are rewarded with wide panoramic views, well worth the invigorating uphill stretches. It is especially interesting because as well as following the Thames towpath we tread two other notable pathways. One is the Ridgeway Path, an officially-designated walkers' route which for most of its length follows ancient trackways that were here when the Romans came. The other is the Icknield Way, the oldest prehistoric trackway in England. Those with a taste for industrial archaeology will enjoy a close-up view of one of Brunel's masterpieces.

Distance: The distance is 7¼ miles, so allow about 3½ hours.

Refreshments: The Perch and Pike in South Stoke and The White House near the half-way mark both offer bar meals and snacks.

How to get there: The starting point is the village of South Stoke which lies just off the B4009, the road running from Goring to meet the A4074 near Crowmarsh Gifford, just across the bridge from Wallingford. It is quite easy to park, discreetly of course, in the village. (OS sheet 174, GR 595 837, but most of the walk is on sheet 175, entering it at GR 600 853).

The Walk: Near the end of the road towards the river take the lane signposted 'Ridgeway Path' and 'To the River'. On coming to the latter, just where the Beetle and Wedge ferry formerly crossed, turn right through a gate onto the towpath.

There are pleasant, if not sensational, views all around while ahead is the sturdy Moulsford railway bridge. As you pass beneath it you realise that it is actually two bridges and that it is a Brunel masterpiece. Its diagonal brick courses make pleasing patterns and the effect, as one stands beneath it, is strangely impressive.

Passing two small tree-covered islands the scenery seems to change in a subtle way. It changes again as you cross a footbridge and trees encroach almost to the water's edge. But when you reach Little Stoke the towpath switches sides. Since we have missed the last ferry by several decades we must take another route a little way inland!

Turn right along the ferry lane (it is signposted 'Ridgeway Path') for about 20 yards and then go left along a path signposted 'Ridgeway Path' and 'Public Footpath to North Stoke'. A stile brings you into a field, the left-hand edge of which you should follow, with the river not far away to the left. Over a concrete footbridge and a stile, and then another stile at the opposite side of a field, the path continues at the left-hand edge of yet another field. At the end of it a stile leads to a path which takes you through a garden to another stile giving onto a grassy area with North Stoke's 13th century St Mary's church to the right. A stile brings you into the churchyard.

Through the lychgate and along a short lane, turn right through the village and then bear left with the road. A little more than a mile of tarmac lies ahead, I'm afraid, yet as it is a quiet country road with hardly any traffic and offering wide views it is by no means unpleasant.

On reaching the B4009, cross to a very minor road opposite signposted 'Ipsden and Stoke Row'. This leads to the A4074 on which you jink right and then left to follow a similarly-worded signpost pointing to the left of a pub called The White House. As this pleasant little road gently climbs you can see, eventually, silhouetted against the sky, a 'Public Bridleway' sign on each side of the road. Turn into the bridleway on the right.

This is the Icknield Way and the going, all the way to a lane, is good.

A small clump of trees conceals a pond directly opposite so this must be circumvented to the left. Then the path goes half right across the field.

Emerging onto the A4074, cross it to a rough, chalky path which climbs to a waymarked gap in the hedge and gives access to a large field. Traverse this in a slightly leftward direction and come to a grassy crossing track on which turn right. On the crest of the hill, a small copse was planted in 1985 in memory of 'Jock' Cameron, 'a highly respected friend and adviser to local farmers for over 40 years'. Enquiries of one of these local farmers elicited the information, omitted from the plaque, that the late Mr Cameron was a Member of the Oxfordshire Agricultural Advisory Committee.

Glorious views open up all around. To the right lies Wallingford, where William the Conqueror and his army, with insurrections to quell, forded the Thames. On a hilltop to the left of the town, the tall beeches of Wittenham Clumps can be easily picked out, marking the site of an ancient hill fort, probably Iron Age. Further left again, stand the unmistakable cooling towers of Didcot power station.

As the path drops to some farm building and then begins to climb again to a copse, its quality underfoot improves. It emerges eventually onto the B4009. Cross, and go along a narrow road signposted to 'Little Stoke'. Where the road bends right, climb over a stone stile to the left of the entrance gates to Littlestoke Manor. (Sometimes Little Stoke is two words, sometimes one.)

Invisibly at first, the path runs at the right-hand edge of a field and crosses a stile and a footbridge. It then weaves clearly across the next field before it bends right, then left, and passes through a tunnel under the railway. It turns left on the other side and then goes half-right across a field, then left towards the houses of South Stoke. When, within a few yards of the first houses, the path forks, take the right fork and enter the village opposite Manor Farm and turn right towards wherever the car is parked.

Historical Notes

South Stoke: One of the most interesting facts about St Andrew's church at South Stoke is that Cromwell stabled horses in it during the siege of Royalist Wallingford during the Civil War. The church dates from the 13th century but was much altered in the 14th. The tower is 15th century. The church thus embraces Early English, Decorated and Perpendicular periods of architecture. In one of the windows is a fragment of 13th century stained glass depicting the Virgin and Child. By the north door can be seen part of a wall painting of the Table of the Law which dates from Elizabethan times.

In Manor Farm's farmyard is the country's second oldest dovecote. Built in the 16th century, it can house about 1,000 pigeons.

Moulsford railway bridge: We saw, on a ramble in Volume I, the great railway bridge at Maidenhead which has the widest and flattest brick arch spans in the world. Also created by the genius of Isambard Kingdom Brunel, the engineer of the Great Western Railway, is the red brick Moulsford bridge. It was built in 1840, the third of his famous brick bridges spanning the Thames; the other is at Basildon. Actually, the Moulsford bridge is two bridges, side by side, connected by small transverse arches.

North Stoke: The church of St Mary the Virgin was built between 1230 and 1240 on the site of earlier churches. Of interest, inside, are a fine Jacobean canopied pulpit and some remarkable 14th century wall paintings discovered during restoration in 1902. They are all around the nave; the Last Judgement is portrayed above the chancel arch and the murder of St Thomas of Canterbury elsewhere. Outside, a mass dial – probably Norman – held in a priest's hands, may be seen over the bricked-up south door. The tower fell down in 1669 and was rebuilt in 1725. The celebrated contralto, Dame Clara Butt, who owned two houses in the village, was buried close to the east end of the church in 1936. Lying with her are her husband and two sons, who both died tragically early.

The Ridgeway Path: The ancient Ridgeway passes through North Stoke. The Ridgeway Path, one of the long-distance routes established following the passing of the National Parks and Access to the Countryside Act of 1949, is an 85 mile signposted chalkland route from Ivinghoe Beacon near Tring to Overton Hill, near Avebury in Wiltshire. The Ridgeway has been walked since the Stone Age.

The Icknield Way runs more or less parallel to the Ridgeway, but at a slightly lower level. Its origin is lost in time but travellers were certainly making their way upon it by 2000 BC. Like the Ridgeway it follows the high ground to avoid marshy areas as well as wolves and other perils.

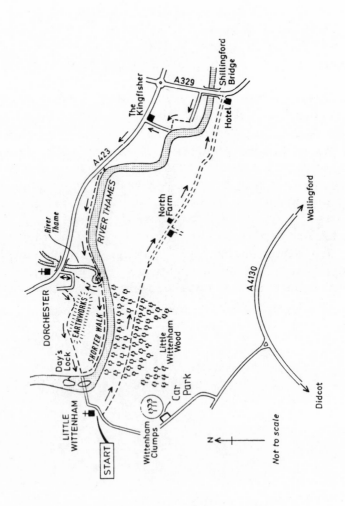

Little Wittenham and Dorchester-on-Thames

Introduction: An opportunity to explore historic Dorchester-on-Thames is one of the attractions of this walk. We shall see, and ponder their purpose, some ancient earthworks, probably dating from the Iron Age. And, remembering as we cross the bridge at the confluence of the river Thame and the Thames that from this point up-river an alternative name of the Thames is the Isis, we may wonder if there is any substance in the theory that the name Thames combines those of Thame and Isis. No difficulties are likely to be encountered apart, perhaps, from a little mud in one or two places.

Distance: The full circuit, including a visit to Dorchester, is 5¾ miles; if you deny yourself this pleasure the walk may be shortened to 5 miles. The full walk would need about 2½ hours.

Refreshments: The Shillingford Bridge Hotel and The Kingfisher around the half-way mark both offer bar meals. In Dorchester there are numerous restaurants and pubs and a tearoom.

How to get there: The starting and finishing point is Little Wittenham which is reached by taking a minor road signposted 'Wittenhams' running north from the A4130 between Wallingford and Didcot and then turning right onto an even more minor road signposted 'Little Wittenham'. Keep ahead when the road forks and park near the church. (OS sheet 164, GR 567 935).

The Walk: Just before the church, and on the opposite side of the road, is a stile leading into a nature reserve, which we shall traverse. Climb over the stile and make your way slightly leftwards across the field towards Little Wittenham Wood – **not** towards Wittenham Clumps, the group of trees high on the rounded hill in front. The path, not very visible on the ground at first, gradually becomes more apparent and you will soon see a stile and small gate leading into the wood. As you gently climb towards it there is a fine view of the river Thames and Day's Lock and weir.

A grassy track goes through the wood which has a wide variety of trees, particularly cypress. When the track splits take the left fork, maintaining your forward direction. After a while the track broadens out and starts slowly to descend. When you finally leave the wood, go forward on the left-hand side of a large field and enjoy good views all around. Soon the buildings of North Farm appear.

The path ends and your way continues along a rough lane. It passes North Farm and at this point the river comes into sight again, away to the left. The lane jinks right and left and in another 10 minutes or so the A329 is reached at the Shillingford Bridge Hotel, a welcome prospect, maybe.

Turn left across the graceful Shillingford bridge which was built in 1830 and is clearly more suited to horse-drawn carriages and carts than to the cars and lorries that thunder over it today. But after only a few yards you can thankfully escape the traffic down a private road to the left, opposite Ferry House. When the road divides take the right fork and immediately enter a footpath to the right. Just past the wall of Shillingford Court a short path to the left leads down to the riverside – a delightful spot for a rest, for which purpose a seat is provided. On a nearby wall is a most interesting scale showing the heights to which the river rose at various times between 1768 and 1929; the terrifying highest was in 1809. Once upon a time, no doubt, this peaceful spot was busy with barges, for the road behind is called Wharf Road.

Regrettably, a short detour is now necessary since there is no right of way beside the next stretch of river. So go up pleasant, grass-bordered Wharf Road, admire the gorgeous wisteria that gives Wisteria Cottage its name and come out on the A423 by The Kingfisher. An unavoidable 6 or 7 minutes' walk, left, on this busy road now lies before you, I am afraid, but fortunately there is a pavement on the right-hand side.

Look out for a stile beside an iron gate on the left – it is just past a road sign saying 'Dorchester' and 'Dorchester Abbey' – which will enable you to cross a field and reach the towpath. Turn right thereon and make your way, through meadows, along a pleasant reach of the river until you come to the footbridge over the river Thame, where it enters the Thames. If you do not wish to visit Dorchester, carry on beside the Thames (a lovely stretch) until you reach Little Wittenham footbridge just before Day's lock – and skip the next two paragraphs.

For the full walk, fork right immediately after crossing the Thame and follow its bank round in almost a semi-circle, then follow the path as it heads across the field to a stile. Beyond it, you pass on the left some ancient earthworks known as the Dyke Hills, and come to another stile. Cross and turn right along the edge of a field. This brings you into a rough lane and soon you join a small road running in front of the Chequers Inn. Turn left. A tunnel by the public conveniences will take you safely under the main road to the entrance to the abbey. I'll leave you now to explore the attractions of the delightful little town. Those who knew it before the bypass was opened a few years ago to divert the heavy traffic that used to shatter its single main street will be agreeably surprised by the peace and quiet now regained.

When you are ready to resume your walk, make your way back to the Chequers Inn and turn right along Watling Lane. Soon, a sign on the **right** saying 'Public Footpath to Day's Lock' points to a footpath on the **left**. Take this path which runs towards the earthworks and, on reaching them, turn right.

Pass over a crossing track and at a 5-bar gate the path bears left between fences. This enchanting path goes through a gate and forward to a footbridge you can see ahead, beyond Day's Lock.

Once over the footbridge there are two more bridges to cross before going up a slight slope and round the corner. And there, by Little Wittenham church, the car awaits.

If you have any energy left a climb to the top of Wittenham Clumps is highly rewarding. The groups of beech trees on top of the hills are a landmark for miles around and therefore a viewpoint for a marvellous panorama of river and country. Here, on the Sinodun Hills, will be found a triple line of banks and ditches of surprising magnitude. When these fortifications were constructed, or by whom, is unknown; most likely they date from the Iron Age although the Romans and Saxons and others undoubtedly utilized them.

They may be reached from the stile at which the walk commenced – but a much easier ascent can be made from the small car park lying beside the minor road on which you approached Little Wittenham; you probably noticed it as you came.

Historical Notes

Little Wittenham: The 'Little' of this hamlet's name describes it well. There is little, too, to be said about it other than that the church contains some brasses and that Day's Lock is smaller than most. Archaeological finds in the neighbourhood suggest that battles, long ago, were fought here, possibly in attempts to take the fortifications on the Sinodun Hills.

Dorchester: In Dorchester your first call will probably be at the marvellous abbey. It is nearly 200 ft long and they say that money ran out before a 19th century 'restoration' was far advanced so that relatively little harm was done. In exploring the ancient small town you follow in the footsteps of the

Romans, the Saxons and the Benedictine monk, St Birinus, a missionary who came from Rome in AD 635 and became the first Bishop of Dorchester. He converted the King of Wessex, baptised him in the river Thame, and went on to make Dorchester as important a Christian centre as Canterbury. Dorchester became the largest diocese in England, embracing what are now the six dioceses of Bath and Wells, Hereford, Lichfield, Salisbury, Winchester and Worcester, which shows how important it was. The abbey dates from 1170. The 14th century Jesse window, with its glass and stone effigies rising around it, is especially renowned. There are numerous monuments of great interest, particularly a crusader's, in the south aisle, which is a remarkable piece of medieval sculpture. The lead font is 12th century.

Dorchester's single main street contains some pleasing old houses, one or two with the upper floors overhanging the pathway. The attractive coaching inn, The George, was possibly the abbey's brewhouse in monastic days.

The two great lines of earthworks known as the Dyke Hills, lying between the Thames and Dorchester, may or may not have been associated in some way with the fortifications on Wittenham Clumps. Little is known of their origin; perhaps they were thrown up by the Romans, perhaps by the Danes, or perhaps they are earlier still. Neither is their purpose clearly understood. Maybe they were military defences – or maybe they were simply defences against flooding.

Wallingford: Although Wallingford is not actually on this walk itself, you may well pass through the town on your way to the starting point or find it convenient to visit afterwards. It is certainly worth spending a while exploring this ancient town, now in Oxfordshire but formerly in Berkshire.

Its charter is one of the oldest, having been granted by Henry II in 1155, the year following his holding of a Parliament there. Earlier, the Romans, the Saxons and the Danes had settlements and remains of Saxon earthworks are still plainly visible. William the Conqueror stayed in the town. The town hall, which dominates the market square and partly conceals St Mary's church dates from the 17th century.

Once there were 14 churches in the town before the Black Death in 1348 wiped out the population so that only 44 families remained alive. That was not the only catastrophe to befall the town. It was ravaged by the Danish King Sweyn in 1006 and a great fire in 1675 destroyed many of its fine old timbered houses. Its castle, built by the Normans in 1071 on the site of a Roman fort, was one of the biggest in England. Little of it now remains.

If you drop down the elegant stairway, half way across the bridge, you will observe from the riverside how the bridge has been altered and added to during its 700 year history. Although it is still so narrow that only one-way modern traffic can be allowed, it was widened at some time in the past. On one side the arches are rounded while on the other side the original pointed arches can still be seen.

The great castle lay to the north-west of the bridge. It was a stronghold that survived many an assault until it was finally destroyed in the Civil War. One of the last Royalist strongholds to surrender, it fell at last to Fairfax. One black day in 1646 Oliver Cromwell, seated upon his horse on Wallingford bridge, watched the execution, one by one, of the whole of the defeated garrison. Their heads and decapitated bodies were hurled into the river, to be borne away on the stream.

Clifton Hampden

Introduction: A short, but quite interesting, walk. There's a sight of one of the minor works of the architect of the Houses of Parliament and a pub with its literary connections with *Three Men in A Boat.*

Distance: The circuit is only 2½ miles so not much more than an hour is needed.

Refreshments: The Barley Mow, which offers food, is opposite the starting point.

How to get there: Clifton Hampden lies partly on the A415 between Dorchester and Abingdon. In the village, turn off the main road onto the minor Little Wittenham road, cross the narrow bridge and park in the free car park just round the bend. (OS Sheet 164, GR 549 953).

The Walk: Clifton Hampden is a picturesque village full of picture-book thatched cottages some of which you will see on the concluding leg of the walk. Leave the car park and turn right past The Barley Mow inn which bears the date 1352 and was made famous by Jerome K Jerome in *Three Men in a Boat.* Cross the bridge, and drop down the little path to the left on the far side of the bridge and then turn right on the towpath.

For a short distance a caravan site on the opposite bank of the river somewhat mars the view but thereafter the whole route is through very pleasant countryside.

Just before reaching Clifton Lock you will notice the divergence of the natural river from the artificial Clifton Cut, which is

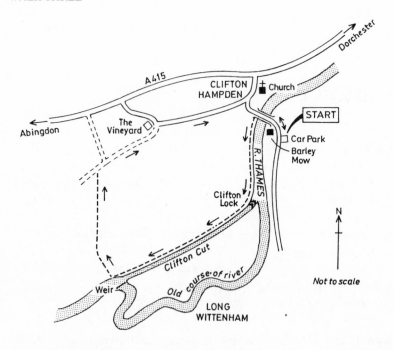

now the navigation channel. For the rest of the waterside section of this ramble you will have the impression of walking beside a canal, as indeed you are. There are no means of following the river's old course, which is a shame, really, for it is very pretty.

Pass, but do not cross, a bridge obviously built to enable the farmer to reach his fields cut off by the construction of the artificial channel.

You reach the end of the cut at the point at which the water tumbles over a weir. Alas, you must leave the waterside here by turning squarely right, across to a stile beside a small iron gate and follow a track running at a right-angle to the river.

Soon you pass from one field to another – and then across another – and then the track goes half-right. At the end of this field the track bends right and its surface improves. Ignore, after a while, a concrete farm road going left and continue ahead. The now sandy way becomes a concrete farm road as you pass farm buildings and approach a fine, weatherboarded house. Behind it, what would once have been a surprising sight on this side of the Channel, is a vineyard.

When you meet a small road at a corner bear right. This wholly delightful road, with its grassy verges and 300 or 400 year old thatched cottages, soon brings you to a road junction where you turn right for a few yards to the bridge, and then the car park.

Before taking the turn to the bridge, however, it is worth while going ahead the short distance to the church of St Michael and All Angels, now much restored, which can be seen ahead perched high on a rock outcrop. From this direction, it is approached up a long flight of steep steps which must surely deter elderly and arthritic worshippers but which nevertheless affords the hale and hearty a remarkable view of the river.

Historical Notes

Clifton Hampden: The seven-arched bridge, best viewed from the towpath, is, in its small way, worthy to stand beside Balmoral and the Houses of Parliament as an example of medieval/Victorian design. Sir Gilbert Scott, no less, was responsible for it. Built in 1864, it was paid for by a local family and replaced a ferry. Jerome K Jerome, after describing The Barley Mow as 'the quaintest, most old-world inn up the river' went on to say 'Its low pitched gables and thatched roof and latticed windows give it quite a story-book appearance, while inside it is even still more once-upon-a-timeyfied'. The inn suffered damage by fire but restoration has been exquisitely accomplished.

Long Wittenham, a neighbouring village, is worth a visit while you are in the vicinity. It is so named because the straight main street is practically a mile long. In the church may be seen the smallest sculptured monument in the country, the ancient stone figure of a knight.

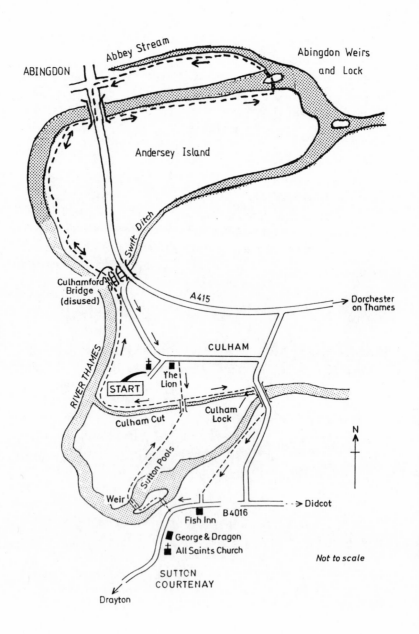

Culham

Introduction: This quite short walk is not only full of interest and beauty but it manages to straddle two counties, for we visit Culham in Oxfordshire and Sutton Courtenay in Berkshire. There is also a 4 mile optional extra walk to Abingdon. I hesitate actually to *urge* you to make this additional hike. Abingdon is an attractive town, well worth a visit, though if you simply want to see it you might as well go there by car after completing the Culham round. Why I hesitate is that our steps along the riverside into Abingdon have unavoidably to be retraced on the way back. This is against all my principles! On the plus side, however, the walk we do after reaching Abingdon bridge is very attractive indeed and I think justifies the effort in getting there and back. But I leave the decision to you.

Distance: The Culham round is 3½ miles. With the extension to Abingdon it is 7½ miles. The full walk would take about 3¾ hours; say 1¾ for the shorter walk.

Refreshments: The Lion at Culham, near the starting and finishing point, offers bar snacks (but not on Sundays) and food may also be had at The Fish Inn at Sutton Courtenay and at the George and Dragon, too, which you will pass if you divert to look at the church. In Abingdon, of course, numerous facilities are to be found.

How to get there: Culham lies about 2 miles south of Abingdon at a junction of three minor roads, two of which run from the Abingdon/Dorchester road (A415) and the other from the

B4016. Park discreetly by St Paul's church which you will find near the end of a little road that crosses the village green from beside The Lion pub. (OS sheet 164, GR 501 950).

The Walk: Notice first the Manor House, opposite the church. This is one of the two exceptional houses this small village boasts. The other is the Georgian Culham House, which can be seen beyond the green through its fine wrought iron gates, a splendidly proportioned edifice.

From the church, make your way back to the road where, the previous time I came this way, the village pillory still stood. A stump of wood is all that now remains. Just past The Lion, turn right along a signposted footpath which leads to Culham Cut, where you turn **left** along the towpath. (Yes, I know. We always walk upstream. But this is not the river, only an artificial cut, dug in 1809. We shall soon be walking along the banks of the real river when we get past Culham Lock which can be seen ahead.) The cut, bypassing a loop in the river and the lovely Sutton Pools which we shall shortly see, was constructed because of the serious obstacle to river traffic posed by a 'flash weir' actually located underneath a mill, a most unusual and awkward arrangement.

Beyond the lock turn right over a bridge and then over the much older Sutton Bridge beneath which flows the Thames in its true channel. After about 100 yards, opposite some cottages, a wooden wicket gate on the right allows you to drop down beside the river. Only for a short distance, however, for soon a hedge on the right obliges the walker to leave the waterside for a while and a stile ahead brings you into a drive. Press on ahead until the drive emerges into a road at Sutton Courtenay and you find yourself facing The Fish inn. You may also note, with relief, that although the path you have just walked is not marked on the map as a right of way it is nonetheless signposted here!

Turn right for a few yards to a corner and then go right down a footpath at the side of Walton House.

First, however, you may care to go left to explore the beautiful village.

Resuming the walk, cross a wooden footbridge to find yourself again following the true course of tne river. Now begins a walk around a backwater which is, without doubt, one of the most fascinating places on the Thames. Cross three metal footbridges over weirs and enjoy views across the wide expanses of water known as Sutton Pools. Finally, cross a larger bridge over the main weir, a spectacular sight and an exciting experience when a lot of water is running.

The path bends right and, over a stile, leads across a meadow to another stile. The path climbs gently towards the bridge over Culham Cut, close to a point passed earlier on; turn left along the towpath on the other side.

To the right you can see the church and Culham Manor again, the latter with its 17th century dovecote with accommodation for 4,000 birds. After about ⅓ mile the cut ends and you find yourself walking once more beside the 'old' river. Almost a mile of very pleasant riverside walking lies ahead until the path meets a road at Tollgate Cottage. Just before reaching it, however, you will notice a rather lovely old wooden footbridge on the left and it is worth diverting the few yards to stand on this bridge. It spans the Swift Ditch which is probably the true main stream of the river Thames. It also gives a delightful view of the 15th century Culhamford Bridge which is no longer in use.

To take the optional extra walk to Abingdon cross this wooden bridge. For the shorter walk skip the next 4 paragraphs.

Follow at the waterside all the way to a stile and gate. The Swift Ditch we crossed is, as mentioned above, probably the real channel of the river Thames; what we are walking beside is almost certainly a 1,000 year old artificial channel. We are also on an island as a glance at the map will show; Andersey Island, it is called. By the time you reach the stile and gate the opposite bank becomes more attractive and an interesting old

iron bridge spanning the entrance to the long-disused Wilts &
Berks Canal will be seen. The inscription upon it reads 'Cast at
Acramans, Bristol. Erected by the Wilts & Berks Canal Com-
pany AD 1824'.

The path is now wide as it passes through a public park. Pass
beneath the bridge and continue near the water's edge. It is a
pleasant walk from here to Abingdon lock. There is a permissive way across the lock, so pass over the gates and continue
along the fenced path on the other side and then over the
weirs.

You now walk beside the Abbey Stream which once served
the great Benedictine monastery of Abingdon, founded in
AD 675. On coming to a new wooden footbridge, recently
erected as a much-needed link in the long-distance Thames
Path, do not cross it but carry on along the delightful path
beside the Abbey Stream with pleasant parkland to the left.
Eventually you will come to a bridge which you should cross
into a car park, turn left and follow the narrow road beside the
remains of ancient monastic buildings and come out through an
archway by St Nicholas church into Market Square. Here I
leave you to enjoy an hour or two in the town.

When you are ready to resume your walk, come back to this
spot, pass down Bridge Street and cross the bridge. Go
through a gap in the wall on the right hand side and drop down
to the path which you walked earlier and retrace your steps to
the wooden bridge over the Swift Ditch. Turn left and come to
the road by Tollgate Cottage.

At Tollgate Cottage, turn right into the road. It is not the
main road but a quiet country road with a path separated by
grass from the carriageway. Didcot power station's giant cooling towers, ahead, do not actually improve the view yet they
are not without a certain grace. In ½ mile you reach Culham's
village green and, turning right where the pillory stood, soon
reach the church and the car.

Historical Notes

Sutton Courtenay, with its wide village street lined with trees, is full of the most picturesque old houses including, in the 12th century Norman Hall, one of the two oldest inhabited houses in Berkshire. Just past the George and Dragon is All Saints' church of various periods and with an interesting Jacobean pulpit and box pews. Three graves in the churchyard are worth searching for. One is of a Mrs Martha Pye who died at the age of 117 in 1822; another is of H H Asquith, 1st Earl of Oxford and Asquith, who lived in the village and who, as Chancellor of the Exchequer, introduced the first provision for old age pensions and became Prime Minister in 1908; the third is of Eric Blair, better known as George Orwell, the author of that horrifying vision of the future, *1984*.

The Swift Ditch is probably the true main stream of the Thames. However, the monks of Abingdon cut a rival channel through the town in the 10th century since the river bypassed the town at that time. They then cut the navigation, by the side of which we walk today, a century later. The Swift Ditch was reopened in 1624 by the Oxford-Burcot Commission who were appointed to improve the navigation below Oxford. The artificial channel through Abingdon, which had become silted up, was dredged and reopened in 1790, thereby bringing traffic back to the town again, and the Swift Ditch was once more abandoned. The Swift Ditch has a claim to fame, however, for one of the first pound locks on the Thames was built upon it.

Abingdon: What we see of modern Abingdon on the other side of the water as we walk beside it round Andersey Island seems unimaginative and characterless, making the contrast with the delightful Old Town when it comes into view as we approach Abingdon bridge all the more impressive. Indeed, we enjoy from our view-point across the water the best possible introduction to what is called the 'Queen of the Thames', with the lofty spire of St Helen's church soaring high above the rows of mellow almshouses. The bridge, originally built in 1416, was rebuilt in 1929.

Like many another town, Abingdon grew up around its monastery, little of which now remains apart from, notably, the Abbey gateway. The splendid Town Hall in the Market Square, Abingdon's centrepiece, was built in the late 17th century by one of Sir Christopher Wren's masons, probably under his master's guidance. St Helen's church, very rare in having five aisles, and being wider than it is long, boasts a 14th century painted ceiling in the Lady Chapel.

The almshouses which grace three sides of the churchyard date from the 15th to the 18th centuries and many half-timbered and fine Georgian houses are to be discovered in the streets roundabout. Abingdon is also an excellent shopping centre.

The Wilts & Berks Canal was built at the end of the 18th century from Semington, where it linked with the Kennet & Avon Canal, to Abingdon, passing through Swindon (this was long before that town acquired the importance the Great Western Railway was to give it) and with branches to Calne, Chippenham and Wantage. It was an expensive canal to construct but at first it made a modest profit carrying coal from Somerset and agricultural traffic. But its fortunes gradually declined in the face of railway competition and it seems almost to have faded away, its channels becoming silted up and un-navigable until it was finally closed in 1914.

Radley

Introduction: Much of this walk passes through the landscape enjoyed by Queen Victoria and her beloved Albert from the bedroom window of their honeymoon retreat. To your astonishment you will find yourself walking – quite legitimately – across the football pitches of Radley College. And you will see the scene of a dramatic event in English history.

Distance: The walk is about 6 miles and could be completed in just under 3 hours.

Refreshments: The Tandem near the start and finish of the walk, The Bowyer Arms half-way round and The King's Arms three-quarters of the way round all offer food.

How to get there: The starting point is Kennington, almost a suburb of Oxford, due south of the city on an unclassified road. A convenient free car park will be found beside the Kennington Health Centre and the Social Club, opposite The Tandem pub. (OS sheet 164, GR 524 024).

The Walk: On leaving the car park go right along the road and, opposite St Swithun's church, turn right into Bagley Wood Road, actually a pleasant country lane. It climbs gently at first. Cross St Swithun's Road to the continuation of Bagley Wood Road opposite but immediately fork right onto a footpath and climb to a playing field. The path now runs, virtually invisibly, along the right-hand edge of the field to a small wooden gate. As you pass through it note, on the stone post, the inscription recording that the playing field you have just passed through is

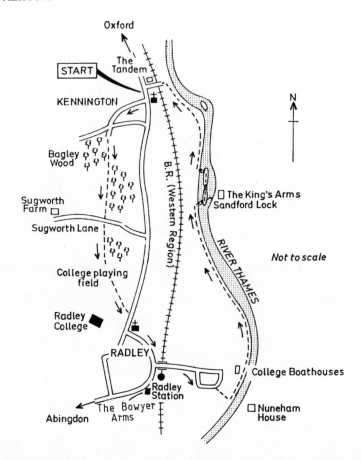

Oxford

The Tandem

START

KENNINGTON

Bagley Wood

B.R. (Western Region)

Sugworth Farm

Sugworth Lane

The King's Arms
Sandford Lock

N

RIVER THAMES

Not to scale

College playing field

Radley College

RADLEY

Radley Station

The Bowyer Arms

Abingdon

College Boathouses

Nuneham House

a memorial to six men who lost their lives in the Second World War.

Keeping right as you drop down towards a wood, you come to a stile and a plank bridge leading over a stream. Your way lies along the main path ahead, just within the boundary of the wood, a delightful path indeed. Although it may be a trifle muddy in places some large stepping stones have been thoughtfully provided in the worst spot. A path joins from the left and another soon after, but ignore them both and carry on ahead. Ignore, too, a footbridge on the right.

On coming to a small road (Sugworth Lane), cross to a gap in the hedge slightly to the right; there used to be a stile opposite. The path, which may not be very plain on the ground, now runs across a large field, slightly leftwards, and skirts the right-hand edge of a small wood before coming to a gap leading onto the Radley College playing field where, surprisingly, the public right of way lies across the football pitches. It is quite invisible on the ground but heads in a slightly leftward direction. Of course, if a game is in progress, the prudent pedestrian will doubtless make his way round the edge of the field! The right of way then passes to the left of a running track, curves right at the end of it then drops down towards a kissing gate in the far right-hand corner. A grassy path leads to a road reached through a kissing gate at a footpath sign (which reassures us that we haven't been trespassing.)

Turn right along the road and come to St James the Great church, on the left. It should be visited, for it is rich in treasures. Turn left into Church Road, then go left over the railway. (First, however, you may wish to go ahead a few yards along Foxborough Road to The Bowyer Arms.) After passing the entrance to a former gravel pit and, later, passing beneath some lofty power lines, turn right at a cream-painted house. The lane soon bends left and, when it begins to bend left again fork right past a house numbered 87. The track bends, runs across a field roughly in the direction of a boathouse, and meets the towpath on which you turn left.

Across the water is Nuneham House, where Victoria and Albert spent their honeymoon, although trees may obscure your view just yet; don't forget to look back over your right shoulder when you have progressed a little further. What you can see from here, however, is the Carfax Conduit in the grounds of the house.

Soon you will pass the extensive premises of the Radley College boathouses. At once, the scenery seems to change, and is quite delightful. Now put this book away and simply enjoy the sights and sounds of the river until you reach Sandford Lock, a good 1½ miles ahead.

A concrete bridge over the weir stream leads to the lock where a permissive way over the lock and a footbridge will take you, if you wish, to The King's Arms where a brass plate fixed half way up the counter in one of the bars shows the level the flood water reached one appalling March day in 1947. To the right, very attractive modern flats now occupy the site of the former Sandford Mill, the mill stream still passing beneath them.

A visit to the pub is a diversion, however. The walk, immediately after crossing the concrete bridge, passes to the left of the lock and along the towpath, crossing two footbridges over weir streams.

Across a metal footbridge, further along, turn right. Then, beyond a gate after about 100 yards, your path goes slightly left over a somewhat marshy meadow, bypassing a loop of the river. Here it was that in the 12th century Matilda (daughter of Henry I, wife of the Holy Roman Emperor, King Henry V of Germany, and rightful Queen of England) escaped the clutches of the usurping Stephen by crossing the frozen Thames after sliding down a rope from her window in Oxford Castle where she had been imprisoned.

To the left you will see a metal footbridge which will take you over the railway. The path, however, goes forward, then curves round towards the bridge. On the other side of the line a road brings you up beside The Tandem. The car park is opposite.

Historical Notes

Kennington is a straggling village. Its importance was, perhaps, greater in the past, when a monastery was established in the 7th century by a nephew of the King of Wessex.

Nuneham House: With a Royal Standard flying directly over their bedroom, Queen Victoria and Albert of Saxe-Coburg-Gotha spent their honeymoon here. Nuneham House was built by the first Earl of Harcourt in the 18th century. It was enlarged in the 19th century and again in the 20th century. The famous Capability Brown was responsible for landscaping the grounds but some of his features were destroyed during the Second World War. The Carfax Conduit, which can readily be seen from the towpath, was originally in Oxford but was removed in 1787 by the Corporation who donated it to the Earl Harcourt who re-erected it as a feature in his garden. Incidentally, when the first Lord Harcourt built the house, on the site of an old manor house, he not only demolished the old house but an entire village too, shifting the inhabitants to a new location on the Dorchester road. This improved his view.

Radley: The church of St James the Great contains some gorgeous Tudor stained glass (and some even older). The most notable is in the west window where Henry VII is depicted in hunting gear. The charming house which is now the vicarage served him as a hunting lodge. The Norman font stands on sculptured legs, each different. The ornate woodwork, acquired by the church in 1653 and which stands behind the pulpit, was formerly part of the Speaker's chair in the House of Commons. The 17th century misericordes in the choir came from Germany and are a reminder that the Anglican religious order called the Community of the Resurrection (now at Mirfield in West Yorkshire) was founded here in Radley by a former vicar, Charles Gore (later Bishop Gore).

St Peter's College, at Radley – generally known simply as 'Radley' – occupies several buildings but is centred round a Queen Anne mansion. In the late 18th century the house belonged to Admiral Sir George Bowyer who lost his fortune in an optimistic, but unavailing, search for coal beneath the estate and was obliged to let the house to a Nonconformist school. This proved little more successful than the mining enterprise, but the premises were acquired in 1847 by Dr Sewell who founded the great public school that stands there today.

Oxford

Introduction: I call this the 'Alice in Wonderland Walk'. That's because the stretch of the Thames beside which we shall be walking between Oxford and Godstow is believed to be that on which Lewis Carroll rowed little Alice Liddell on the afternoon of 4th July 1862 and began to weave his immortal story. It is an interesting and easy walk, on good paths throughout and all on much the same level. Also it is by the waterside for most of the way, for we go out along the river Thames and back along the Oxford Canal. I must confess, however, that what we see of the canal today, as it passes through suburban and industrial parts of the city, does not show the fair face it reveals when it meanders through the countryside further north, where it boasts a reputation as the country's second most popular pleasure-cruising canal. But it is interesting, and the walk beside the Thames is pleasant indeed. The Thames takes several channels through Oxford and no one knows which is the true one. In times past numerous cuts were constructed to serve watermills. What seems today to be the main channel, and the one we follow, was probably dug by the monks of Osney Abbey to power their mill.

Distance: About 5¼ miles which could be completed in 3 hours at a leisurely place.

Refreshments: Plenty. At Binsey there's The Perch Inn, at Godstow The Trout Inn, in Wolvercote (facing each other) The Red Lion and The White Hart while, beside the canal, there is The Plough just over Bridge No 236 and The Anchor near Bridge No 240. All offer food. Facilites of every kind can be found, of course, in Oxford.

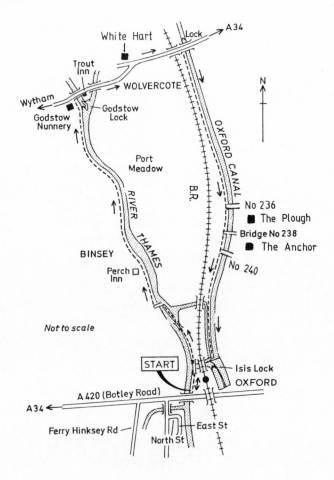

How to get there: You don't need me to tell you how to find Oxford, I'm sure. The only difficulty likely to be encountered before you start walking is trying to find somewhere to park. The starting point of our ramble is Osney bridge over the Thames west of Oxford railway station. Just west of the bridge which is on the Botley Road (A420), is a small bridge with 'Osney Town' on it and immediately left, over this bridge, is North Street with 24 hour parking for a few cars. If all else fails there will certainly be space in Ferry Hinksey Road (sign-posted 'Osney Mead Industrial Estate') at traffic lights a little further along Botley Road, but this will add ten minutes or so to your walking time. (OS sheet 164, GR 503 063).

The Walk: The starting point for the walk is the north-east corner of Osney Bridge where a little slope drops down to the towpath. The first couple of hundred yards or so run beside garden fences but the houses are soon left behind when you cross a graceful iron footbridge over the entrance to the cut linking the river to the canal. Astonishingly – as if a curtain had been lifted – you are immediately in open country and there is water on either side.

After some distance you pass over a bridge, ignoring a bridge on the right which leads into Port Meadow and to the Medley boat station. Soon the towpath ends on this side of the river, so cross to the other bank by a footbridge which, according to the inscription, was erected by public subscription in 1865. There must have been a ferry here when Carroll and Alice came this way.

Resume your direction. The river broadens at this point and the great Port Meadow comes into view, 439 acres of common land held by the freemen of Oxford since before the time of Edward the Confessor. Keep beside the water and, after passing through a couple of gates, you will see the tiny group of cottages at Binsey. Pass (or not pass, as the case may be!) a stile on the left inviting a diversion to The Perch Inn at Binsey; the thatched hostelry is much closer to the river than the cottages observed just now.

Continue along the towpath and come, eventually, to God-stow Lock. Turn round here for a glance at Oxford's distant 'dreaming spires'. Then you come to the ruins of Godstow Nunnery, founded in 1133 and inhabited at first by the widows and unmarried female relatives of Norman kings and nobles.

The towpath meets the road at the narrow double-arched Godstow bridge. Cross the bridge carefully and come to the delightful old Trout Inn, formerly the guest house of the nunnery, with its terrace patrolled by a peacock, overlooking the weir. Make your way along Godstow Road and come to a bridge over a mill stream. Just on the other side of this bridge is a touching memorial to two young officers of the Royal Flying Corps who were killed when their monoplane crashed 100 yards from this spot on 10th September 1912; touching, but interesting, with its pictorial representation of the flimsy aircraft.

Follow the road round to the left and then right, through Wolvercote, then left and right again; the pubs are about here. Further along the road ahead (it is still called Godstow Road) you will pass beside Wolvercote Common. Make sure you cross the road to its left-hand side before you reach the railway bridge; you'll see why when you get there. Immediately beyond the railway bridge, drop down a steep path on the left to the canal towpath. There is a lock here, but diminutive compared with the big Thames locks you have seen. Turn right.

When you reach it, Bridge No 238 will turn out to be of an interesting type common on the canals – a lifting bridge. Heavy as they are these bridges are usually easy to operate, being so nicely balanced.

Eventually, after passing a weir and a turning basin, you reach the elegant bridge No 243 by Isis Lock. Do not cross this bridge, however, but go over a less elegant one on the right which takes you onto the towpath beside the connecting cut between canal and river. You will notice a now disused, and permanently closed, railway swing bridge. Opening and closing it was a laborious task and, over the years, this swing bridge has been cursed by boatmen and railwaymen alike.

All but the shortest walkers will have to stoop to pass beneath the next bridge and then you are beside the Thames again. Turn left at the footbridge and soon you are back where you started, at Osney Bridge. This area seems to be rich in awkward or low bridges, for Osney Bridge (you will not be surprised to learn when you look at it from the towpath) has the lowest headroom of any on the navigable length of the river.

Historical Notes

Oxford is too big, too important and too well-known for me to be able to do it justice in the space available here. So I'll simply recommend you to call at the Tourist Information Office where you will find maps, folders and books to tell you all you might want to know about this fascinating city's many attractions and places of interest.

The Oxford Canal: Boats first reached Oxford on the length of canal by which we walk today just 200 years ago, in 1790. The Oxford Canal, authorised in 1769, was one of the first to be built in England. Three years earlier the Trent & Mersey Canal had been authorised, to link those two rivers by way of the Potteries. While it was being built, the Coventry Canal and the Oxford Canal were projected, which together would join the Trent & Mersey to the Thames and to London. Building of the Oxford Canal started at the northern end, at Hawkesbury, near Coventry. It reached Napton in 1775, Banbury in 1778 and Oxford in 1790. The rivers Trent, Mersey and Thames were thus joined so all of them could serve London. During the next few years a great deal of traffic passed, borne in traditional narrow boats. But in 1805 a new, shorter route was opened: the Grand Junction (now Grand Union) Canal from Braunston to Brentford and a short cut to Birmingham through the new Napton Canal and Warwick Canal. This drained much of the traffic from the lower part of the Oxford Canal between Napton and Oxford. In 1937 the basin and wharf in Oxford were sold to Lord Nuffield. The site was filled in and Nuffield College stands there now.

Godstow Nunnery: See notes at the end of Walk 7.

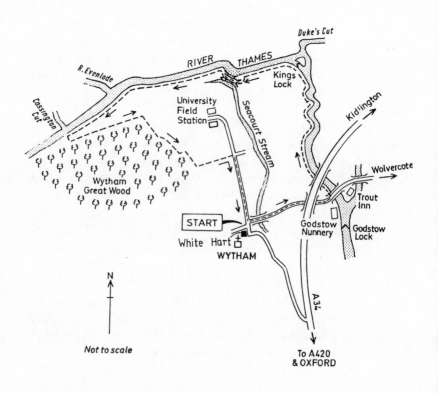

Duke's Cut

RIVER   THAMES

R. Evenlode

Cassington Cut

Kings Lock

University
Field
Station

Seacourt Stream

Kidlington

Wolvercote

Wytham
Great Wood

Trout
Inn

START

Godstow
Nunnery

Godstow
Lock

White   Hart
WYTHAM

A34

N

To A420
& OXFORD

Not to scale

Wytham

Introduction: This walk has the advantage of following the river bank for a delightfully long stretch. It starts in the delightful village of Wytham, the golden stone of whose cottages, many thatched, suggest that we are not now far from the Cotswolds.

Distance: About 5¼ miles, which could be completed in 2½ hours at a leisurely pace.

Refreshments: At Wytham is The White Hart and at Godstow, 10 minutes after the start, The Trout Inn. Also, at Wytham, teas may probably be served in the garden of the stores and post office during the summer months.

How to get there: Wytham lies on a minor road that leaves the Oxford ring road (A34) about a mile north of the intersection with the A420. Alternatively, it can be approached by a minor road from Wolvercote which passes underneath the A34. There are several odd corners in the village where you may park discreetly. (OS sheet 164, GR 475 087).

The Walk: This ramble starts with 10 minutes' walking on a road out of Wytham signposted 'Godstow and Wolvercote'. Actually there is a narrow path running between hedges to the right of the road and parallel with it but this is so overgrown that you might not think it worth while. There is little traffic on this quiet road.

47

Just before reaching the Thames at Godstow bridge you will pass the ruined Godstow Nunnery, founded in 1133 and generously supported by the Norman kings and noblemen as a convenient retreat for their widows and unmarried womenfolk. You may care to know, if you didn't visit the White Hart before you started and now wish you had, that the fine old inn called The Trout, which was formerly the Nunnery's guesthouse, is just over the bridge. It has a pleasant garden, patrolled by a peacock, and overlooks the weir stream. The bridge is horribly narrow; it is also, I believe, tricky for boats to navigate.

However, if you do not cross the bridge, turn left onto the towpath by a sign saying 'Eynsham 4 miles'. The towpath soon passes beneath the A34. At a point, shortly reached, where the river makes a sharp bend to the right, many walkers no doubt take a short cut over the meadow towards King's Lock (the weir machinery of which can be seen ahead) thereby avoiding two loops in the river.

Carry on past the lock, above which is Duke's Cut, a connection with the Oxford Canal. Cross a footbridge over the weir on the Seacourt Stream which was passed over earlier on the road out of Wytham – and you now see that it is not a small river as you probably then thought, but an outflow from the Thames. (It rejoins the river in Oxford.) Immediately another short cut, avoiding another loop in the river, may tempt you. From now onwards there is not always a clear path and much of the way is over grass. But if you keep near the water's edge you can't go wrong.

As you pass it, you can see on the other side of the river the confluence of the river Evenlode and then, a little later, an old canal. This is the disused Cassington Cut on which barges used to bring corn to Cassington Mill. Here we leave the riverside. Exactly opposite the Cassington Cut – at the point where Wytham Great Wood comes down almost to the water's edge – turn sharply left and follow round the right-hand boundary of the field with a barbed wire fence and the wood on your right.

For a short distance you will find yourself walking parallel with the towpath on which you have come.

It is not much of a path that you now follow but the going is quite easy and if you keep close to the fence all will be well. Press on until you come to the end of this side of the wood. Still carry on as near to the fence as you can, although the path for the next 180 yards is not easy to discern on the ground. And then you will see, over a waymarked stile, a long, straight cart-track on the right, going between fields towards a distant part of the wood. There's an interesting notice affixed to the stile. It reads: 'University of Oxford – Experimental field margins. These margins are part of a long-term experiment to improve the conservation of wildlife on farmland. Please keep to the track. Do not walk on the grassy field margins or move the marker canes.' For the greater part of the rest of the walk you will be skirting the fields cultivated by the University Field Station.

Follow the track, which gently rises. When the wood is reached the track bears slightly left but when, after 60 yards, it sweeps away to the left over the field, continue on the waymarked path ahead, keeping close to the fence and the trees.

You come to a ditch and the path does a sharp turn to the left to a small, railway-sleeper bridge which takes you over a ditch to a stile. Having crossed this, proceed up the right-hand edge of a field to another stile. Beyond this a narrow bridge crosses another ditch and the path goes on at the right-hand edge of another field. At the end of this field the path bears slightly left but immediately crosses another ditch and you pass through the hedge onto a wide track. Turn left and follow this all the way to a crossing lane and turn right in this for the short distance back into Wytham where the walk began.

Historical Notes

Wytham: The big house at Wytham, within its 700 acre park, is not visible from the road. Although it is called Wytham Abbey there never was an abbey here. The tiny All Saints' church was rebuilt in 1811 by the 5th Earl of Abingdon as part of his alterations to the estate. Materials from the earlier church were utilised as well as stone from the ruinous house which had been a grange of the monks of Abingdon. A church has stood on the site since the 12th century at least. A curious feature is the small window glimpsed at floor level beneath the 17th century 'holy table'. The main east window has some fine 17th century Flemish glass; elsewhere is glass from the 14th century.

Godstow Nunnery: Of the nunnery, a Benedictine foundation of the 12th century, all that now remains are the walled enclosure and the shell of a small chapel. The story that chiefly adheres to the nunnery is that of 'Fair Rosamund' – the beautiful and witty Rosamund de Clifford who was educated there and who became the mistress of King Henry II. He kept her for several years at his palace at Woodstock, where he concealed her in a secret bower which, he imagined, was secure against intruders. But his jealous queen, Eleanor of Aquitaine, found her way in one day and offered her rival a cup of poisoned wine – or so legend has it. Certainly Rosamund died soon after. She was buried in a magnificent tomb in the choir at Godstow but the Bishop of Lincoln, on a visitation, ordered 'Take the harlot hence and bury her without the church'. The Fair Rosamund had been a favourite, however, even of the nuns. So, although they removed her body from the church, they reinterred her in the chapter-house next door.

Northmoor

Introduction: A very pleasant walk, all on much the same level. Exactly half of the walk is beside the river and a delightful stretch it is, too. It is a peaceful walk in rural countryside for once the village of Northmoor is left behind only three points of human habitation are passed, Northmoor Lock, a farm and The Rose Revived inn. A few anglers, minding their own business at the water's edge may be the only people you see.

Distance: A circuit of 5 miles which would take about 2½ hours.

Refreshments: In Northmoor village are The Red Lion and The Dun Cow. The first is quite near the starting point and both of them will be passed as you near the end of your walk. The Rose Revived at Newbridge is reached around the two-thirds mark. All offer bar meals.

How to get there: Make for Newbridge where the A415 crosses the Thames about half way between Abingdon and Witney and take the minor road (Moreton Lane) beside The Rose Revived inn. This leads, in 1½ miles, direct to Northmoor where, at a T-junction, turn right and park near the church. (OS sheet 164, GR 421 029).

The Walk: From the church, carry on ahead along the road – or along a little path parallel to it on the right, until it ends. Then cross a stile, right, by a gate and a footpath sign, and make your way along a wide stony track, passing through pleasant

51

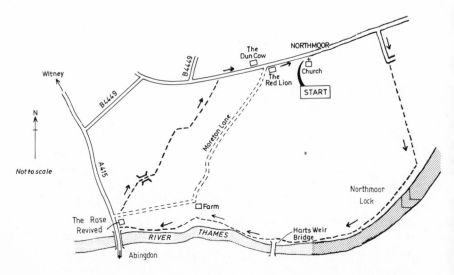

open country. When the stony track turns sharply left, and ends, carry on ahead along a grassy track and come to a concrete bridge and a gate. Go through it and follow the not very visible path ahead and reach the towing path on which turn right. The other side of the river is splendidly wooded.

A lovely long stretch of delightful riverside walking now lies ahead. Come to, and pass, Northmoor Lock. Cross a small, gated bridge over a tributary stream and come, after some distance to Harts Weir Bridge. Do not cross it. Cross a stile and carry on along the towpath. Pass through a wooden gate where the river bank is contained by a short length of walling and there is a farm to the right. Carry on between wooden fencing and then along again at the riverside.

Over a little concrete bridge the path takes a short cut to avoid the river's bend. A splendid view of the ancient bridge, paradoxically called 'New' bridge, opens up.

Our way goes through the riverside garden of The Rose Revived inn and up to the road. Turn right here for a few yards and into Moreton Lane beside the inn. After another very few yards, a footpath sign will be seen on the left indicating

'Northmoor 1½ miles'. Climb the gate and cross the field, half-right (the 'finger' on the signpost points the direction) and come to a wooden bridge over a stream, and cross this.

After a few yards, the path bends left and merges with another coming from the right. Pass through a narrow band of trees. Cross over the next field, heading somewhat to the left of a power pylon. Join a gravelly track which soon bends right then twists and turns a little before heading straight towards the road. You can't go wrong. And when you reach the road, in which you turn right, you will see a footpath sign pointing back the way you have come. A ½ mile or so on this road will bring you into Northmoor again, passing The Dun Cow on the left and The Red Lion on the right before you reach your car.

Historical Notes

Northmoor: Like many another Thames-side village, North-moor lies well back from the river, beyond the flood-lands. The 14th century church is notable for an early 18th century singers' gallery and a bell loft which was occupied by musicians, instead of an organ, until quite recent times. A tombstone has a reference to the Great Plague of London of 1665. There are some fine old stone cottages in the village.

Northmoor Lock: Here, for the first time on our Thames-side rambles, we encounter a weir that still retains the paddle construction of earlier weirs. Before the introduction of pound locks a number of paddles in a weir would be lifted to make an opening through which the water, which had been held back, surged. When its force had sufficiently abated boats would be enabled, somewhat perilously, to pass.

Harts Weir Bridge: This isolated footbridge is on the site of an old flash weir. A public right of way, dangerous as it un-doubtedly was, was evidently established across the weir and although the weir has long gone, the right of way, now across the bridge, has been maintained.

A tale is told hereabouts of Betty, the lovely daughter of the humble weir-keeper, who caught the eye of William Flower, 2nd Viscount Ashbrook, then a student at Oxford. They were married in 1766 in Northmoor church. After a very happy, but short, married life Betty was left a widow. But after only a few years she married a distinguished Oxford theologian and one of her great grand-daughters married the 2nd Duke of Marlborough, ancestor of Winston Churchill.

Newbridge

Introduction: Newbridge, at the centre of this ramble is the location of what is widely regarded as one of the loveliest inns on the Thames. It also has historical associations, being the site of a fierce skirmish during the Civil War. Trousers may be a good idea to guard against any nettles or brambles, as parts of the riverside path may become overgrown.

Distance: Allow 2 to 2½ hours for this 4½ mile walk.

Refreshments: On one side of the bridge at Newbridge is The Maybush, on the other side, The Rose Revived. At Longworth, in Tuck's Lane, is The Blue Boar. All offer bar food.

How to get there: The starting point is the village of Longworth, which may be reached along any one of several minor roads running north from the A420 about 9 miles south-west of Oxford. Park discreetly near the eastern end of the village, perhaps in the side road named Bow Bank and signposted 'Longworth School' (OS sheet 164, GR 391 993).

The Walk: Start walking from the eastern end of the village where, at Rodney Place, the road swings right in the direction of the main road, and go ahead along a private road which a notice describes as a public footpath. When the tarmac ends and the track splits into three, take the centre one, slightly left, and carry on with a large field on the left and soon on the right as well, until you reach a farm. Here the track turns sharply left, but go right to pass the farm buildings on a grassy path and soon come to a signposted bridleway where you turn left.

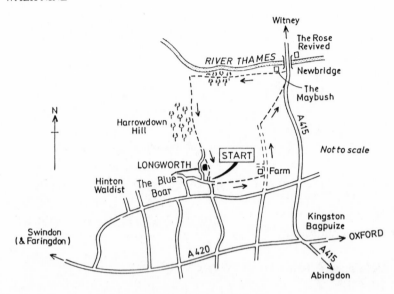

The way is metalled until the farm is passed, then fork right along a sandy lane. At a junction of three bridleways turn right through a 6-bar tubular metal gate (your way being indicated by one of the signs) and proceed along the left-hand edge of a field towards another gate. Through this, your way continues as before near the left-hand edge of a field until, at the top of it, a metal gate leads into the A415 road in which you should turn left. Walk on the grassy verge as the road is curved and the traffic fast.

But not for long. In 200 to 300 yards you reach the Thames at the narrow bridge, one of the oldest on the river. Access to the towpath is gained along a path at the side of The Maybush. The first part of the riverside walk lies at the edge of wide fields but after a while you reach a stretch where trees and bushes have grown up beside the water. After a few yards a waymark sign directs you toward the edge of the water; from here the path through the greenery may be found overgrown and a little difficult. I note, however, that a path has been trodden out beside the field, skirting the overgrown section. **This is not the right of way** but is clearly much used, all the way to the end of the overgrown section.

The 'proper' path, when it emerges from the trees, comes to a footbridge with a gate at either end. Leave the riverside here and bear left towards a stile in the barbed wire fence. This gives access to a path which comes to a tiny hump-back bridge and climbs to a field – at the point where the 'unofficial' path joins it from the left.

The path now runs at the right-hand edge of a field, slowly climbing towards tree-clad Harrowdown Hill and at the top of the field a gate brings you to a track which you cross. The way continues ahead, between hedges along a more or less straight – but maybe muddy – path running up and over the hill. A splendid view opens up to the left.

Coming out into a lane by the entrance to a house called Tucksmead, turn left in the lane and bear right with it. At Glebe Cottage cross its drive to a signposted footpath on which you make your way at the right-hand side of a field. At the top of it the path bends right round the side of a playing field and leads into Bow Bank, the road in which you probably parked your car.

Historical Notes

Longworth: Among Longworth's attractive houses are the Old Rectory, chiefly Georgian but partly Tudor, and the Manor House. The village's chief claim to fame is as the birthplace of John Fell (1625–1686), scholar and prelate, who is forever remembered through a well-known quatrain composed by one of his students at Oxford, Tom Brown:

> 'I do not love thee, Dr Fell,
> The reason why I cannot tell;
> But this I know, and know full well,
> I do not love thee, Dr Fell.'

Brown is believed to have composed the verse when Fell promised to rescind the youth's expulsion order if he could make an impromptu translation of the Latin epigram:

'Non amo te, Sabidi, nec possum dicere quare;
Hoc tantum possum dicere non amo te.'

Newbridge: Despite its name, the bridge at Newbridge is probably the second oldest on the Thames, its senior being Radcot. Originally built in the mid 13th century, it was reconstructed 200 years later. Notwithstanding its antiquity, it still copes gamely with the heavy traffic that thunders over it today. Much blood was spilt upon it in a fierce skirmish during the Civil War when Royalist troops repulsed a Parliamentary attempt to move on Faringdon, held for the king.

Tadpole Bridge

Introduction: Definitely among the book's Top Ten walks, this is a delightful ramble through marvellously peaceful and remote countryside and along a particularly attractive reach of the Thames. I've done this walk twice. Except for the landlord and a couple of other customers in the pub by the bridge (which I visited only on the first round) I met but one person on the two occasions.

Distance: About 3 hours would be needed to complete the round of 6¾ miles.

Refreshments: Only at The Trout Inn, conveniently situated almost exactly at the mid-point, where bar meals may be obtained.

How to get there: Running north from the A420 about half way between Oxford and Swindon is a minor road signposted 'Littleworth and Thrupp'. Drive carefully through Littleworth and drive down a long and narrow, but very straight, road. After nearly 1½ miles it bends sharply left, near a very big electricity pylon. (A lane continues ahead.) There is room, just round the bend, to park off the road on the grassy verge. This is the starting point. (OS sheet 164, GR 301 991).

The Walk: Retrace your steps round the bend and after 100 yards turn left into a lane signposted 'Bridleway'. There are thick hedges on either side of the lane but through gaps in it you can glimpse agreeable views of a pastoral landscape. Pass

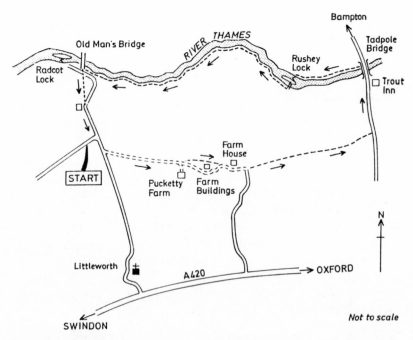

Brixton Farm and, later on, just over a cattle grid, Pucketty Farm, lying back to the right. Somewhere around here the lane becomes more of a track. After passing a wooden gate across the track, the right of way (waymarked) diverges leftwards from the track to bypass a house and stables and comes to a wooden footbridge.

Beyond this, the path runs across a field to a gate that can be seen ahead, passing approximately 100 yards to the left of red-brick farm buildings and through an iron gate. (It's a bit muddy around here.) The path then crosses the next field, not far from the hedge on the right, heading very slightly to the right of a farmhouse ahead, and emerges through a 6-bar tubular metal gate back onto the track (or perhaps one should say 'lane' again now) at a bend.

Carry on along the lane (not the track running toward the farm) and pass the farm on your left. At a corner, where the lane bends sharply right, bear slightly left at a double 'Bridle-way' sign, pass a group of delightful cottages and through a wooden gate. Despite the sign, the bridleway is not much to look at on the ground, but it goes along the left-hand edge of the field. Ignore a small stile you may notice on your left.

The view to the right gets more and more attractive. The path jinks right, then left, and continues along the left-hand edge of the great field at the end of which you come to a crossing track. Continue ahead, jinking slightly right, to pass along the left-hand edge of yet another field. Then, through an opening in the hedge at the end of the field, the path goes **across** the next field, heading at first more or less directly towards a large house ahead. But when the next field is reached, through a metal gate, the path runs at the right-hand edge of the field and comes to a gate leading into a road.

Turn left for ½ mile or so to Tadpole Bridge. I'm sorry about this unavoidable bit of road walking but it's a fairly quiet and quite picturesque country road. And when you come to the bridge over the Thames you are rewarded, for beside it stands The Trout Inn, a welcome sight maybe.

Cross the fine bridge, which is nearly 200 years old, and go down left onto the towpath, now upgraded to a National Rivers Authority road as far as Rushey Lock. The river banks are high above the water here and colourful with a rich variety of wild flowers. You reach the lock through a gate on the left. There is a permissive way over the lock gates and, by passing to the left of the lock-keeper's cottage, to the weir. This weir, which is one of the few (like Northmoor) which still retain the paddle construction of weirs of an earlier age, will fascinate any reader who has an interest in inland navigation. In the mind's eye one can soon gain a picture of how a 'flash' weir operated before pound locks were introduced.

Over the weir, turn right along the towpath, through a gate and shortly across a footbridge over a stream. No matter where one looks along the next stretch to Old Man's Bridge and, indeed, almost all the way back to the car, there is not a glimpse of any human habitation.

From here to Old Man's Bridge, along what I think is one of the most delightful reaches of the river to be found in this book, the Thames twists and turns. One ought, I suppose, to resist the temptation to take short cuts. The well-trodden path, however, has no such misgivings. I shall not attempt to describe all its contortions over the next couple of miles. If you keep the river somewhere on your right you won't get lost.

Pass what looks like two ancient burial mounds, the first one partly demolished at the time of writing. They are not marked as such on the 1:50,000 Ordnance Survey map. Shortly, you will notice a small bridge with wooden railings to your left. It is actually the bridge which carries the little road from Radcot Lock to more populous parts; don't go towards it. Ahead, and slightly to the right, is a large footbridge called Old Man's Bridge and you make towards it, but do not cross it.

(If you wish to make a short diversion to Radcot Lock carry on along the towpath and then come back to this point.)

Turn your back squarely to Old Man's Bridge, then walk ahead near the right-hand edge of the meadow, a hedge on your right, along a path that at first is not very visible on the ground. Come, eventually, to a stile and cross it. (The little road from the lock converges just here.) Turn left along the lane, which soon bends right and then goes straight ahead to join the road at the bend by your starting point.

Historical Notes

The bridges: The narrowness of the river allowed it to be spanned by Tadpole Bridge with a single arch. The elegant stone bridge was constructed in 1802. Like Harts Weir Bridge (Walk 8) Old Man's Bridge is on the site of an old flash weir. A public right of way having been established across the weir, a bridge had to be provided when the weir was removed so that the public's right might be maintained. If, when you get back to the car, you care to drive west along the road for a couple of miles to the A4095 and turn right thereon for another 1½ miles, you will come to Radcot Bridge, almost certainly the oldest on the Thames. The piers may be 12th century or even older while the two outer arches are probably 14th century and the centre one probably later. Tradition has it that all three arches were originally pointed but that the centre one was rebuilt, rounded, after being damaged during a fierce battle fought here in 1387 in the course of a rebellion against King Richard II. The centre arch still carries the base of a cross. Cavalier and Roundhead blood was spilt here more than once during the Civil War.

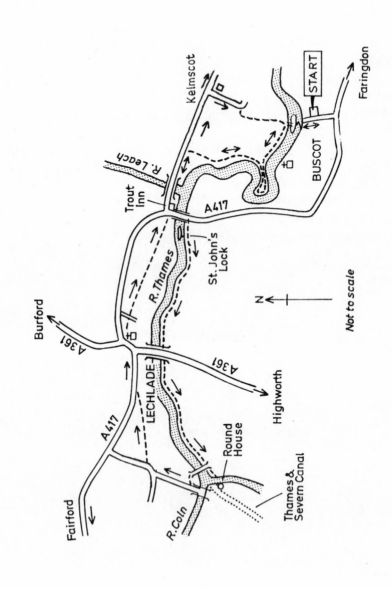

START

Faringdon

Kelmscot

R. Leach

Trout Inn

A417

St. John's Lock

R. Thames

BUSCOT

Burford

A361

LECHLADE

A417

A361

Highworth

Fairford

R. Coln

Round House

Thames & Severn Canal

N

Not to scale

Lechlade

Introduction: This is a very pleasant ramble in the countryside around one of the most attractive Thames-side towns. Lechlade is the highest point to which the Thames was navigable by commercial vessels and so, a mile above the town, the towpath ends. (Once upon a time navigation could have continued along the Thames and Severn Canal – but that's another story.) On our subsequent rambles we shall no longer have the towpath to tread, but instead we shall enjoy walking some delightful Thames-side paths.

Distance: A circuit of some 5½ miles which will comfortably fill 3 hours. The less energetic among us can, if they wish, shorten it to 4 miles.

Refreshments: Near the starting point is The Apple Tree; the Trout Inn will be passed on the way out and on the way back. Both offer bar food. In Lechlade itself there are various facilities including tea rooms.

How to get there: Our starting point is the pretty village of Buscot, which lies to the north of the A417 a couple of miles on the Faringdon side of Lechlade. Turn right in the village, just before The Apple Tree, and you will find on the right-hand side the National Trust's free Buscot Weir car park. Park here. (OS sheet 163, GR 231 976).

The Walk: On leaving the car park turn right along the lane through part of the 4,000 acres the National Trust owns around these parts. When the lane forks, take the right-hand route and cross a small bridge. Immediately turn right along a signposted footpath to the lock and weir. The path leads over a footbridge above a weir, over the lock gates (across which there is a permissive way) and then over a bridge above another weir. Pass through a wooden gate and turn left along the towpath, with wide meadows ahead. Erosion seems to have brought the towpath to an end for a while, but keep along at the water's edge.

When the river makes a deep loop you will probably find yourself following the short cut that ramblers' feet have trodden out to bypass it. Soon, however, you must leave the riverside for a while so, where the river bends slightly left, pass through a wicket gate beside a metal farm gate. A very pleasant track then brings you to a little road in which you turn left. Take your bearings here for you pass this way again later.

At a T-junction, just after crossing the river Leach which gives Lechlade its name, turn left past The Trout Inn and over St John's bridge; there has been a bridge here for 700 years. A gate and some steps on the right go down to St John's lock, the highest lock on the river. Beside the lock reclines the bearded figure of Father Thames, a statue commissioned in 1854 for the Crystal Palace and presented to the Thames Conservators in 1958. At first they stationed it at the river's source in Trewbury Mead, but prudently translated it to this hopefully more vandal-free location in 1974.

Once past the lock you are on the towpath again and make your way towards Lechlade's Halfpenny Bridge, so named because that was the sum exacted as a toll from pedestrians until 1839. Pass through a tunnel beneath the bridge and those wishing only to undertake the shorter walk now turn left, up the steps and over the bridge into the town – to rejoin the rest of us four paragraphs ahead. We will rendezvous by St Lawrence's parish church.

The more energetic of us continue along the towpath for a mile through parklike countryside to a sturdy footbridge spanning the river. Don't cross it, however, until you have walked along the last few yards of the towpath to the Round House which stands sentinel at what used to be the entrance to the Thames and Severn Canal that linked our two greatest rivers. What you might at first think was the canal, on the other side of the river is, in fact, the river Coln which here joins the Thames. The canal, which seems to have been filled in, went off beside the Round House.

Retrace your steps to the footbridge, cross it and proceed along a path beside the Coln and into a drive. Turn right and, on reaching a lane, turn right again. Then, when the lane immediately bends left, go ahead over a stile and follow the path beside a hedge on the left. The path that now lies ahead crosses more stiles than I have ever encountered in such a short distance; 11 altogether (I think)!

Maintain your direction across fields, slightly leftwards, over stile after stile until the path reaches a stile leading into a path between houses. A final stile – a stone one, for a change – gives onto a road. Turn right for a few yards into the centre of Lechlade.

The short cut comes in here. Take Shelley's Path on the north side of the parish church and, at the end of the church-yard, cross Wharf Lane and continue on the path opposite. This is a very ancient path which linked the church with St John's Priory, dissolved even before the Reformation. You will come out on the road close to The Trout Inn and cross to the Kelmscot road opposite. Not far along this road you come to the gate through which you emerged earlier – at the point where I invited you to take your bearings.

You now have a choice. You can retrace your steps along the riverside to Buscot lock – and things always look different when viewed from another direction. Alternatively, you can come with me on another way back to the lock, a less pictur-esque route, but slightly shorter.

Carry on along the road for a short distance then turn right into the entrance to Leaze Farm Dairy Unit (just short of a house) and follow the farm track all the way to a stream where, slightly to the right, a new footbridge crosses it. A second footbridge follows and then the path goes half left across a field to a stile leading to the lock.

After crossing the bridges over the weirs and the lockgates, make your way up the track to the car park.

Historical Notes

Lechlade, which takes its name from the river Leach – which we cross on our walk – is an ancient town. It was important in earlier times both as a marketing centre and because it was on a coaching route to London. The 18th century New Inn is a fine coaching house. Some splendid old houses contribute to the town's charm, the 17th century Church House, adjoining the churchyard, is perhaps the most impressive. The church of St Lawrence, whose tall spire is a landmark for miles around, is said to be one of the six finest parish churches in Gloucester-shire. Its 15th century Perpendicular style is all of a piece, with no structural additions or changes in the last 400 years. The stone of which it is built was brought from Taynton and is the same as was brought to Lachlade and shipped down the Thames to London to be used in the building of St paul's Cathedral. At the north side of the church is Shelley's Path, so called because it was here, in 1815, that Percy Bysshe Shelley composed *A Summer Evening, Churchyard, Lechlade*; 'Here could I hope . . . that death did hide from human sight sweet secrets', are words from the poem, inscribed on a tablet embedded in the wall of this lovely churchyard.

The Thames and Severn Canal: Although a link between the two great rivers had been contemplated for a long time it was not until 1789 that the canal was opened. Its enabling Act of Parliament, it is amusing to note, specifically reserved to the canal not only the water from any springs in its bed but also 'such rainwater as fell on its surface'! But no doubt its proprietors were glad of every drop of water they could get for the canal was to lose, through the Great Oolite of its summit level, 3 million gallons of water a day. The canal's 30 miles, including a branch to Cirencester, took seven years to complete at a cost of more than £200,000. A substantial proportion of that sum was sunk in the construction of Sapperton Tunnel (over 2 miles long and the third longest in Britain) and the 16 locks that lifted the waterway to the tunnel and down the Golden Valley to Stroud where it joined the Stroudwater Navigation which in turn joined the Severn. As can be imagined, there was great jubilation in Lechlade when the first boat arrived; a dinner at five of the principal inns, the ringing of bells, a bonfire, a ball and a 12-cannon salute. Yet fortune never smiled on this union between Tamesis and the fair Sabrina. As long ago as 1862 only nine vessels entered the Thames from the canal in the first five months of the year. By 1927 it was derelict.

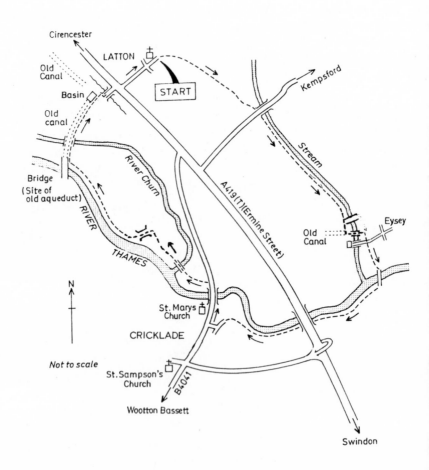

Cirencester

LATTON

Old Canal

Basin

Old canal

START

Kempsford

Stream

Bridge (Site of old aqueduct)

RIVER CHURN

A419 (T) (Ermine Street)

RIVER THAMES

Old Canal

Eysey

N

St. Marys Church

CRICKLADE

Not to scale

St. Sampson's Church

B4041

Wootton Bassett

Swindon

Cricklade

Introduction: Cricklade is an important point on the river for, just as Lechlade marks the highest place to which commercial craft could navigate the Thames, so Cricklade is just about the highest point that can be reached by pleasure craft except, maybe, canoes. The river hereabouts is little more than a large stream. You may find the odd muddy patches on the walk. But they present no real difficulties and there are interesting things to be seen, especially by the canal enthusiast and, in a notable nature reserve, by the botanist.

Distance: The circuit is 5¼ miles, which should take 2½ to 3 hours.

Refreshments: Only in Cricklade, rather more than half way round, where there are restaurants, pubs and cafés.

How to get there: The starting point is the village of Latton, which is on the A419(T) Swindon to Cirencester road about 5 miles south of Cirencester. A 'Latton' sign appears beside the road at each end of the village but the main part of it, including the church, is along a presently unsignposted road called Gosditch running north-east from the main road at a decapitated medieval 'preaching cross' standing in a tiny grassy island. Take this minor road and park near the church. (OS sheet 163, GR 094 958).

The Walk: Start walking along the lane at the south side of the church and come, at the end of the made-up section, to a large metal gate with a clear, fenced path beside it on the left. Do not take this path, however, but pass through the gate and then through a wooden one on the right. The path, or rather the line of it, for it is quite invisible on the ground, runs in a slightly leftwards direction towards a wooden gate that can be seen in the hedge at the far side.

The gate has a small gate beside it which one could formerly pass through but both are presently so dilapidated that you must climb over. Proceed along the right-hand side of the field. Cross a stile – or go through a gate beside it – and continue your direction along the right-hand side of the next field to another stile. Beyond this, the path still goes on at the right-hand side of the field until, at the end of it, you cross a double stile – that is to say, one stile straddling two fences – and come out into a narrow road.

A footpath sign opposite points to Eisey (it is 'Eysey' on the map) and Calcott. Follow the path – a cart track, actually – on the right-hand side of a stream. Curiously, the Ordnance map shows the right of way as being on the other bank, but there is no path over there and the signpost certainly indicates the path we are following. After passing a tubular metal gate the way becomes indistinct but keep about the same distance from the stream as before.

It is a moot point whether the true right of way moves to the other bank of the stream from a small footbridge reached shortly before the end of this path. Yet as the way to the bridge is obstructed by a permanent fence I carried on along the path we are on.

Pass another iron gate and you find yourself crossing a levelled out bit of the Thames & Severn Canal. Immediately, cross a stile on your left and then a footbridge and come to a triple signpost, the arm with 'Latton' on it pointing to the path from which you would have emerged had you crossed the obstructed footbridge just now. Now follow the path indicated by the signpost as towards Calcott and Cricklade, to the right. The path leads over a stile, across a lane in front of a cottage and continues opposite along the left bank of the stream; the path is rather poor and may be a little overgrown but it is quite short and you soon reach a stile beyond which is a field in which it is very easy to walk. Ignore the perilous-looking bridge over the stream at this point; if we had had to cross this I would have 'scrubbed' the whole walk!

Make towards a metal footbridge to be plainly seen slightly to the left ahead and you will find that we have at last reached the Thames.

On the other side of the river turn right beside it. Shortly climb a stile, and then another. Cross a concrete footbridge over a tributary stream and continue with the Thames on the right. Just before reaching the main road climb another stile and pass beneath the road. Cross another stile, then a footbridge over another stream and make your way along any one of half a dozen paths towards Cricklade, still with the Thames on the right.

A stile by a gate (probably open) takes you out of the field. Now, be careful. Don't go ahead by a concrete causeway but go along the right-hand edge of the small field to a stone stile in the corner of it and cross into a rough lane where you should turn left.

After a few yards turn right into Abingdon Court Lane which leads into Cricklade's main street. Turn right, unless you wish first to explore this attractive town or to find one of its refreshment places.

The walk continues down the main street, past St Mary's church, a basically Norman building which had become redundant as an Anglican place of worship and has returned, most interestingly, to Roman Catholic use. Bear left with the road and cross the bridge over the Thames. Then, just before reaching a slightly humped bridge, leave the road by a stile, left, at a footpath sign. The path goes half right across a field to a gate in the corner where you reach the riverside once more and cross a footbridge over the river Churn where it enters the Thames. Rising at Seven Springs, near Cheltenham, this unimpressive little river is the highest source of Thames water.

Now you are in Cricklade's North Meadow, a nature reserve which is one of the finest examples of ancient meadow in Britain. It is noted for its rich plant life which is maintained by haymaking and subsequent grazing.

The path through the meadow takes you a short distance inland from the river but when a narrow wooden footbridge over a ditch is reached on the left, cross it, and cross the field towards the river but do not cross a bridge over it; instead turn right along its bank. Through a wooden gate reached before long you carry on along the path at the riverside and, at a stile beside a gate, re-enter the North Meadow nature reserve.

Next, you will come to a farm bridge on the site of a former canal aqueduct which carried the North Wilts Canal over the river. Climb up to, and over, a stile by the bridge but do not cross it. Turn right along the path ahead and through the trees – the old canal towpath. The canal itself, completely dried out, appears as an indentation on the left. A large wooden foot-bridge takes you over the river Churn again and to a stile. Beyond this, and despite the clear path ahead, the right of way (according to the map) switches to the other side of the canal. Since there is no water in it this presents no problem. But common usage clearly favours the path on the side you are already on. And, since it comes to a stile in a barbed wire fence which crosses the canal and obstructs the way on the other side, it seems we are encouraged to stay on the side where we are.

The path jinks right, then left and gives a wonderful view of a lovely old canal aqueduct. Cross a footbridge and a stile brings you into a drive. Carry on ahead, and eventually emerge into the main road. Turn right for a few yards then cross and go left by the 'preaching cross' into Latton village where you left your car.

Historical Notes

Cricklade was the site of a Roman settlement and there are traces of a defensive bank and ditch around the town which were probably constructed by King Alfred. Cricklade is said to have been a seat of learning in the 7th century, 500 years before the University of Oxford was founded. The church, dedicated to St Sampson, a Welsh-Breton saint, has a four-pinnacled tower built in the 16th century which dominates the countryside for miles around. Of Saxon origin, the church was extended by the Normans and altered in all the periods after, until the tower was built. A 14th century churchyard cross stands outside St Mary's church which is basically Norman and has been recently restored to Roman Catholic worship.

The North Wilts Canal: It is hard to believe that this little waterway, beside the dried out bed of which we walk today, was quite important in its time. Opened in 1819 it ran from a basin on the Thames & Severn Canal at Latton to join the Wilts & Berks Canal near Swindon. By allowing traffic bound for London – principally coal – to reach the Thames at Abingdon instead of at Lechlade, the shallower and longer navigation of the upper reaches of the river was avoided. Indeed, the poor state of the upper reaches of the Thames, and the frequent difficulty of navigating them, were factors which contributed to the ill-fortunes of the Thames & Severn Canal. (See the Historical Notes to Walk 11 for further information about the Thames & Severn Canal.)

Latton: Sited as it is beside the Roman Ermine Street, Latton has ancient origins. Roman coins have been found in the vicinity. St John the Baptist's church has a tower the lower part of which is solidly Norman, as is the doorway. The chancel, however, beyond its grand Norman arch, was rebuilt twice in the 19th century. The 17th century oak bench pews filling the nave and transepts are all of a piece.

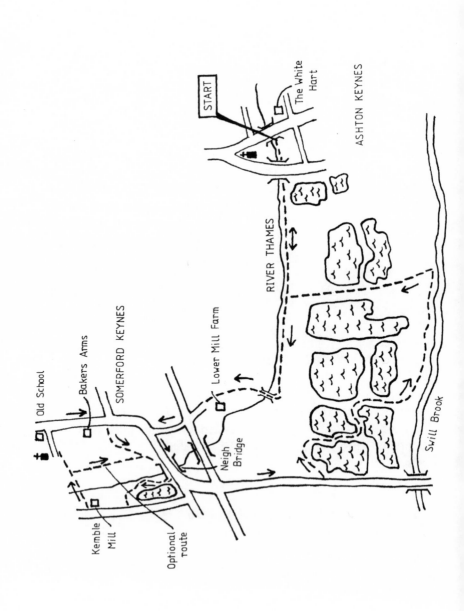

Ashton Keynes

Introduction: A walk beside what may certaintly be termed the 'Infant Thames' and beside a stream called the Swill Brook which, actually, is rather more impressive than the Thames around these parts! Near Somerford Keynes we tread a new path, a wholly delightful one, recently established in the Neigh Bridge Country Park. And later on, we explore a corner of the Cotswold Water Park.

Distance: The circuit is about 6½ miles so a little over 3 hours should be sufficient. An optional diversion avoiding the village of Somerford Keynes will shorten the walk by about ⅔ mile.

Refreshments: Just by the starting (and finishing) point in Ashton Keynes is a pub called The White Hart and at around the mid-point in Somerford Keynes is The Bakers Arms. Both offer bar meals.

How to get there: Ashton Keynes lies at the junction of several unclassified roads. It is about 4½ miles almost due south of Cirencester from which it may be reached on a road through Siddington. Its nearest approach from a main road is from the B4040 between Cricklade and Malmesbury, along a minor road going north from a junction about 3 miles from Cricklade. Or you can get to Ashton Keynes on a minor road running south-west from the A419 between Cirencester and Cricklade about 34 miles from Cirencester (OS sheet 163, GR 045 942).

The Walk: Park discreetly as near as possible to the old village cross which, although decapitated (Cromwell's vandals, possibly) stands by the entrance to Church Walk. Turn into Church Walk and cross an ancient stone bridge. Church Walk is a lovely little road with some desirable houses and with the Thames, only a few feet wide, gently flowing on the right. A bridge across it leads to the church, standing some distance off, but do not go that way unless to visit the church and that is something you might find more convenient to do on your return to the village.

Your way is ahead, along a path between houses and beside the river. A road is shortly reached. Cross it and carry on again beside the river with a lake now on the left. Across a wooden footbridge the scene becomes particularly charming.

Pass over a sandy road and ignore a footpath sign pointing right over a narrow bridge. Soon, when a stile is reached and a triple footpath sign, follow the Somerford Keynes direction. **Note**, however, that proposals are afoot at the time of writing for the creation of a holiday village in this vicinity. If this comes about the path may be diverted here to the opposite side of the river. So follow any diversion signs and maintain your direction.

There are now lakes on either side and, on the left, the Lower Mill Nature Reserve (No Admittance). Ignore a concrete bridge over the river. Soon the path curves to a footbridge over the river and, across it, turn left along a sandy track with the river now on the left and the Lower Mill Country Park on the right.

Carry on past Lower Mill Farm and along the lane ahead. Before long the Thames bends away to the left leaving only a small stream to walk beside. Cross a road and continue along the lane opposite which is fenced off against vehicles just here and enter the outskirts of Somerford Keynes.

On coming to another road turn left into it, leaving the houses behind. After only a short distance cross a bridge (Neigh Bridge) over the Thames and immediately drop down right to a grassy path beside the river. (This new path, through the Country Park, may not yet be shown on the Ordnance map.) Soon another lake comes into view and our path, more distinct now, climbs a knoll between lake and river. Eventually, the path goes left across the concrete-bagged head of the lake and emerges into a lane in which you turn right.

The entrance to Kemble Mill is soon reached and a footpath sign pointing to Somerford Keynes. This is your way. Enter the path over a footbridge and, past the old mill house, three little bridges which bring you to a stile. A double footpath sign then appears on the right. One arm points across the fields to Somerford Keynes and the other to Neigh Bridge.

(If you do not wish to visit the village, its church and pub, you can go this way to Neigh Bridge: cross a stile and make your way, left, along the edge of a field. It takes you across a narrow bridge and a stile and beside a stream all the way to a ladder stile which leads into the road by Neigh Bridge. Here, you'll rendezvous with those of us who have been to the village. Skip the next two paragraphs.)

For the main walk going into Somerford Keynes follow the direction pointed by the signpost's arm across the field. On reaching the far side of the field a small footbridge brings you into another field which you cross, slightly leftwards, towards a gate to the right of the church. Through a kissing gate turn right – unless you first visit the church – and at the end of the path turn left into the village street and then right along it, shortly coming to The Bakers Arms on the right.

Continue through this attractive village and, just before reaching a road on the left signposted to Ashton Keynes and Cricklade, turn into a very narrow path (easily missed) on the right. The path runs between a fence and a hedge and, after 100 yards or so, cross another stile of sorts and a narrow bridge over a stream. Turn left and follow the bank of the stream all the way to a ladder stile which brings you to the road at Neigh Bridge. Here we meet up with those who followed the route avoiding the village.

Cross the bridge – for the second time.

Go left with the road as it bends; don't take the road ahead into the Country Park. Cross the main road and make your way along the lane opposite, signposted to Minety. There is a lake on either side as you follow this very straight lane for exactly ½ mile to a point where a stile stands on each side of the lane. Cross the one on the left and, obeying the injunction carved upon it, to 'keep to edge of field', immediately turn left, the path skirting a lake on the right. Cross another stile beyond which the path bends sharply right by a notice bidding the walker to avoid disturbing wildlife and farm animals. The gravelled path bends sometimes right and sometimes left and there are lakes on either side. Eventually the path crosses a bridge; turn right. When the track you are now upon bends left, go ahead to the right of a lake on a grassy area on which the path, although waymarked, is not visible on the ground.

Cross a stile and continue ahead, bearing left round the edge of the lake and with the Swill Brook coming into view on the right. You are separated from the brook at first by a wire fence but when the fence ends you can follow a path near the bank of the stream. Past a clump of small trees, to pass which you have come a few feet inland, the path bears rightwards, beside the stream again. Cross a stile and a footbridge and carry on beside the Swill Brook but when the way ahead is barred by a fence, turn left beside it, as indicated by a waymark. Go right with the fence as it turns, then left as indicated again by waymarks. Cross a stile, beyond which the path is gravelled for a while and then becomes a track. Cross a stile – and you find yourself by the triple signpost you noticed earlier on the walk. Turn right and retrace your steps into Ashton Keynes, the Thames on your left.

A small diversion may be made on the way back, if you wish. Instead of crossing the last road you come to before reaching the village, turn left along it the short distance to Holy Cross church which you can see. It is well worth a visit. On emerging from the church, turn left along a pleasant, curved path into Ashton Keynes.

Historical Notes

Ashton Keynes: William Cobbett, on one of his *Rural Rides*, came upon Ashton Keynes and decided it must once have been a large market town. He called it 'a very curious place'. We would rather call it a very attractive place, with its houses of lovely honey-coloured Cotswold stone and with many tiny bridges spanning the stream between the garden gates and the road. The stone cross near which we start our walk is only one of four crosses the village possesses. When or why they were erected nobody knows. The tops of all four were smashed by Cromwell's troops during the Civil War but the missing stones of the churchyard cross were discovered in the village in 1917 and reinstated. This cross was then dedicated as a war memorial on 25th July of that year, a year before the end of hostilities. Was it, one wonders, the country's first Great War memorial?

The appropriately named Holy Cross church is largely 13th century and Perpendicular but the chancel arch is Norman. Perhaps, however, one should say **was** Norman for during the alterations in the 1870s the arch was dismantled and re-erected wider and higher, so that its stones are now a mixture of Norman and Victorian. On the former stones can still be seen marks made by the Norman masons. The chancel is strangely, and quite beautifully, decorated, its decorations having been restored and cleaned by church members in 1976.

The war memorial is not the only reminder of human tragedy. There is another, and a very modern one, too. In the tower arch at the west end of the church is a glorious engraved glass screen given in memory of a young lady of the parish and her fiancé who were about to be married when they lost their lives in the Zeebrugge ferry disaster. They are buried together in the churchyard.

Somerford Keynes: A church was built here about AD 700, probably by St Aldhelm, Abbot of Malmesbury; the door of this church can still be seen in the north wall. Five hundred years later the greater part of the present church was built by the Keynes family. The tower was erected in the early 1700s. Drastic restoration was undertaken in 1875–1876 by Frederick Waller, a leading church architect, who – it sounds incredible – pulled down the roof and most of the outer walls and scrapped the gallery, pews and pulpit and replaced some Tudor windows with Victorian ones. Yet it must be admitted that the church is pleasantly uncluttered and full of light. The pulpit of 1876 is particularly interesting, being of artificial Coade stone, the secret of the manufacture of which has been lost. The church and manor house make a pleasing group. The latter is basically 15th or 16th century with later additions. The very existence of Lower Mill and Kemble Mill – not to mention the former mill above Ewen which is even nearer the river's source, prove that the Thames must once have been a much mightier stream hereabouts than it is today.

Cotswold Water Park; The Cotswold Water Park consists of two areas of lakes which have been formed around Ashton Keynes and South Cerney in the west section, and Fairford and Lechlade in the east, as a result of gravel extraction. Out of a total of nearly 100 lakes there are more than 70 in the Ashton Keynes section. Many are still in the process of being worked for sand and gravel but of those where extraction has been completed a variety of recreational activities are being developed by private owners and the local authorities through the Cotswold Water Park Joint Committee. In addition to providing all sorts of water-based activities, there are also two public country parks and a number of picnic sites as well as a network of public footpaths and bridleways.

Somerford Keynes

Introduction: This walk starts and finishes in Somerford Keynes, an attractive Cotswold village clustering around its church and manor house. It is a pleasant easy ramble, being mostly all on the same level throughout. The countryside through which it passes is pleasing if not spectacular; at least, it more than compensates for the Thames being a somewhat unimpressive sight around these parts. In fact, it comes as a surprise to find the river (which, actually, is in an artificial channel, dug many years ago) so narrow and sluggish. Yet one reads that once upon a time the highest water mill on the Thames was at Ewen, which we visit along the way while Upper Mill Farm, which pass on this ramble, clearly takes its name from yet another mill, long gone.

Distance: The circuit is about 4½ miles, so allow 2½ to 3 hours.

Refreshments: At Somerford Keynes is The Bakers Arms and at Ewen The Wild Duck; both offer food. The Wild Duck particularly advertises afternoon teas.

How to get there: Somerford Keynes lies at the junction of several unclassified roads. It is 2½ miles south-east of Kemble, or 4 miles due south of Cirencester, from which it may be reached on a road through Siddington. It is about equidistant from the B4040 between Cricklade and Malmesbury and the A419(T) between Cricklade and Cirencester. From either main road follow signs, in the first instance, to Ashton Keynes. Park discreetly in the village. There is a very convenient grassy

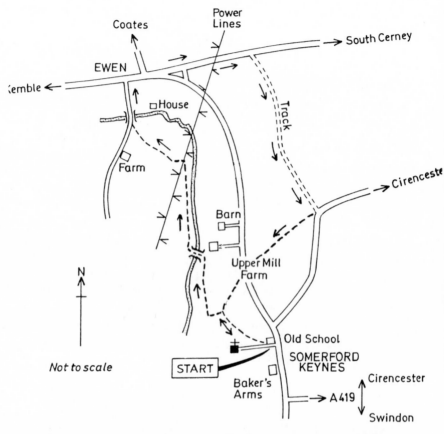

verge at the beginning of the 'No Through Road' which turns off towards the church by the old school. (OS Sheet 163, GR 018 955).

The Walk: Immediately beyond the old school, at a stone stile, a signposted public footpath begins – as does our walk. Not very plainly on the ground, the path runs half left across the field towards a stone-built cottage and to a field gate behind it, which becomes visible as you approach. Beside it is by far the narrowest stile I have ever seen. After you have squeezed over it the path then runs half right across another field to a pair of wooden gates with a conventional stile beside them. Over this stile, the path goes ahead for just a few yards to a footpath sign where you have to do a sharp left turn to another stile beside a gate in the hedge.

Over the stile turn right, along the edge of a field. At the end of the field cross a stile by the side of double metal gates and cross the next field half right towards farm buildings. Before reaching them, however, the path bends left, heading toward the left-hand side of the farmhouse and a stile beside a footpath sign. Cross the stile, turn left and cross a wooden footbridge – over the Thames, no less! – and turn right along rather a rough footpath beside it. Cross another stile and carry on in the same direction as before. Pass, but do not cross, an obviously very old double arched bridge over the river.

Cross another stile and after a couple of hundred yards, another, where a waymark directs us left – almost exactly in the direction of a distant church spire. The path, invisible on the ground, then goes half right across the field. Aim towards a point about 100 yards to the right of farm buildings ahead. Through a gate, the way goes ahead towards a stile at a footpath sign lying roughly mid-way between the farmhouse on the left and a rather lovely old house on the right. The stile leads directly to an ancient (but reinforced) stone bridge over the Thames.

Cross the bridge and make your way the short distance up the lane to the hamlet of Ewen and turn right at the T-junction. Ignore the turning for Siddington and Coates and bend left with the road when a 'No Entry' lane comes in ahead. Pass (or maybe not pass!) The Wild Duck Inn, ignoring the minor road to the left of it but noticing a very curious, modern wooden wayside cross.

Some unavoidable road walking follows as you leave the village. Two hundred yards after passing a house on your right and then a house on your left, turn right along a rough track and carry on along it until you reach a quiet, country road. Turn right at the road, but only for a very few yards. On the right you will see a footpath sign saying 'Somerford Keynes 1 mile' and a stile; this is the way to go.

With a hedge on the right, make your way along the right-hand edge of the field, climbing slightly, and come to a small road. Cross it diagonally, right, to a stile, over which you follow the waymarked direction, on a curving path, half left, over the next field and come to a stile which you will recognise as one you crossed on the way out. You will know where you are now. Cross the stile, and go half left across the field to emerge – after crossing one more field – just where you parked the car.

Historical Notes

Somerford Keynes: See the Notes to Walk 13.

Ewen: A delightful hamlet which remains much as described in books written four centuries ago. Its splendid hostelry, The Wild Duck Inn, is its most notable building and is possibly where John Leland stayed on one of his journeys. Leland was chaplain and librarian to Henry VIII and bore the title Royal Antiquary. He was given the task, for six years, of travelling the country to seek out objects of antiquity in the archives and libraries of cathedrals, abbeys and priories.

The Source

Introduction: In a sense, this walk has found its way into the book by false pretences for, unlike all the others, it is not circular although, on the way back, you can make a small diversion if you wish. Yet the source of the river Thames simply must be included. It is, of course, what all the walks in the book have been aimed towards!

Yet one approaches the source of the Thames with mixed feelings. There is the satisfaction of having at last reached journey's end, but there is also the nagging doubt as to whether this really is the source. Thames Head in Trewsbury Mead, which we shall visit today, is considered by most authorities, ancient and modern, to be the river's true source. Here, for many years, stood the statue of Old Father Thames which has lately been removed to St John's Lock near Lechlade, where we saw it on Walk 11. But the odd thing is that hardly a drop of water ever rises here!

Distance: It takes rather less than 2 hours to complete this ramble of 3¾ miles.

Refreshments: A short diversion on the way back from the river's source may be made to The Thames Head Inn, where food is obtainable.

How to get there: Our walk starts from a point on the A429 about ½ mile from Kemble in the Cirencester direction. Just past a farm there is a small, rough, unsigned layby on each side of the road and a footpath sign on each side, too. These laybys

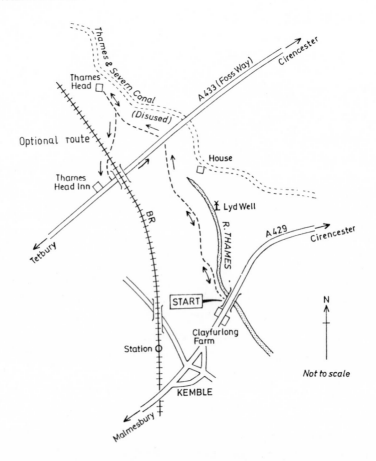

are actually on the bridge which carries the road over the usually dry bed of the river Thames. (OS Sheet 163, GR 991 979).

The Walk: Go over the stile beside the gate on the left-hand side of the road (with your back towards Kemble). Do not take the clear path curving away to the left but walk as near to the riverside as possible – by 'riverside' I mean the indentation in the ground where the river would be if there were any water. Carry on beside the 'river' for a while until the path, which is probably not very plain on the ground, runs over the field in the direction of a 12 ft length of fence blocking a gap in the hedge. On reaching this point turn right along a grassy track with the hedge on your left. The track goes through a gate by a footpath sign. Over to your right you will see a wind pump. Below it is Lyd Well, possibly of Roman origin, a spring which at certain times of the year produces the first Thames water.

Continue ahead, with a hedge on the left, and notice to the right a slight dip in the ground marking the line of the Thames.

Almost opposite a rather nice house of Cotswold stone the path bears right and crosses the bed of the Thames at a point where some stones lying around seem possibly to be the remains of an old bridge. The path now runs towards a stone stile – not the easiest stile in the world to climb – which leads into a road, the A433, the Roman Foss Way. An extremely lofty and therefore hopefully vandal-proof footpath sign pinpoints the spot from a distance.

Having carefully crossed the road, which has become somewhat busier since the legions left, you can see, lying back from the road, an iron gate which gives access to a field. The path follows the left-hand side of it and comes to another iron gate leading into Trewsbury Mead, a field enclosed by a beautiful drystone wall.

A track goes ahead across the Mead towards a stone block – maybe you can see it in the distance – surrounded by trees. You will find inscribed upon it: 'The Conservators of the River Thames 1857–1974. This stone was placed here to mark the source of the River Thames'. As mentioned above, there formerly stood here a splendid statue of the bearded figure of Father Thames, but this has been prudently moved to a safer resting place beside St John's Lock at Lechlade. Well – this is it. The source of England's greatest river!

A few loose stones lie around, indicating the spring where, occasionally, a little water rises. At one time there was a large well here, with water sufficient for the needs of the Roman garrison camped on the nearby mound called Trewsbury Castle.

It has been alleged that the construction at the end of the 18th century of the Thames & Severn Canal, now derelict, which passes a few yards above where we stand, probably had something to do with the present paucity of water since it was a canal which depended upon pumping for its water supply and it was near here that water was pumped to the canal's summit level from underground springs. But a water shortage was reported earlier than that.

The geography of this area is such that I found it impossible to plan a circular walk to include the source of the Thames, so I can only invite you to turn round and go back the way you came, which isn't as bad as it sounds for the scenery always looks different from the opposite direction. And if you go to take a close look at Lyd Well you will notice that there seems to be a permissive path from there along the 'river' bank to the bridge where your car is parked, and that will make a slight variation.

If, however, the prospect of visiting The Thames Head Inn attracts you, the necessary diversion is as follows. It has two disadvantages, however; it means a walk on a very busy road and the negotiation of a dangerously narrow bridge through which drivers are enjoined by a notice to drive slowly. The notice is plain enough to pedestrians like you and me but seemingly invisible to most motorists.

Start back from Thames head in the direction in which you came, towards the gate in the drystone wall, but divert towards a stile beside a small wooden gate in the corner of the Mead to the right of the iron gate. Through this, a grassy path climbs slightly and comes to a stile giving access to a crossing of the railway. With the utmost care, cross the railway lines. On the other side, climb a stile and, with the railway on your left, make your way along a broad track which widens out with many kinds of wild flowers in profusion all around. (At least, that's how it was the previous time I came this way, though most of this area, which was apparently formerly a railway goods yard, seems now to be a resting place for old lorries!)

Leave the area by a kissing gate and come out onto the busy Foss Way, or A433. Just to the right is The Thames Head Inn. Your direction after leaving the inn, however, is left, under the railway. Exercise extreme care here for the road is busy and the bridge narrow. Keep along the road until you come to the stone stile beside the very lofty footpath sign. You know the way back from there.

Historical Notes

Source of the Thames: Thames Head is the official one, of that there is no doubt, but the truth is that the Thames is served by more than one spring. Seven Springs, 3 miles from Cheltenham, is perhaps the strongest rival contender and a stone tablet stands there inscribed '*Hic Tuus O Tamisine Pater Septemgeminus Fons*' which, translated, means 'Here, O Father Thames, is your sevenfold fount'. Yet although the Seven Springs may be the highest source of Thames water, they feed the river Churn which is but a tributary of the Thames.